Edexcel GCSE (9-1)

History

Spain and the 'New World', c1490–c1555

Series Editor: Angela Leonard   Author: Rosemary Rees

Pearson

Published by Pearson Education Limited, 80 Strand, London WC2R 0RL.

www.pearsonschoolsandfecolleges.co.uk

Copies of official specifications for all Edexcel qualifications may be found on the website: www.edexcel.com

Text © Pearson Education Limited 2017

Series editor: Angela Leonard
Designed by Colin Tilley Loughrey, Pearson Education Limited
Typeset by Phoenix Photosetting, Chatham, Kent
Original illustrations © Pearson Education Limited
Illustrated by KJA Artists Illustration Agency and Phoenix Photosetting, Chatham, Kent.

Cover design by Colin Tilley Loughrey
Cover photo © Alamy Images: Robert Harding Picture Library Ltd

The right of Rosemary Rees to be identified as author of this work has been asserted by her in accordance with the Copyright, Designs and Patents Act 1988.

First published 2017

19 18 17
10 9 8 7 6 5 4 3 2 1

British Library Cataloguing in Publication Data
A catalogue record for this book is available from the British Library.
ISBN 978 1 292 12728 6

Printed in Slovakia by Neografia

A note from the publisher
In order to ensure that this resource offers high-quality support for the associated Pearson qualification, it has been through a review process by the awarding body. This process confirms that this resource fully covers the teaching and learning content of the specification or part of a specification at which it is aimed. It also confirms that it demonstrates an appropriate balance between the development of subject skills, knowledge and understanding, in addition to preparation for assessment.

Endorsement does not cover any guidance on assessment activities or processes (e.g. practice questions or advice on how to answer assessment questions), included in the resource nor does it prescribe any particular approach to the teaching or delivery of a related course.

While the publishers have made every attempt to ensure that advice on the qualification and its assessment is accurate, the official specification and associated assessment guidance materials are the only authoritative source of information and should always be referred to for definitive guidance.

Pearson examiners have not contributed to any sections in this resource relevant to examination papers for which they have responsibility.

Examiners will not use endorsed resources as a source of material for any assessment set by Pearson.

Endorsement of a resource does not mean that the resource is required to achieve this Pearson qualification, nor does it mean that it is the only suitable material available to support the qualification, and any resource lists produced by the awarding body shall include this and other appropriate resources.

Websites
Pearson Education Limited is not responsible for the content of any external internet sites. It is essential for tutors to preview each website before using it in class so as to ensure that the URL is still accurate, relevant and appropriate. We suggest that tutors bookmark useful websites and consider enabling students to access them through the school/college intranet.

Contents

How to use this book

What's covered?

This book covers the Period Study on Spain and the 'New World', c1490–c1555. This unit makes up 20% of your GCSE course, and will be examined in Paper 2.

Period studies cover a specific period of time of around 50 years, and require you to know about and be able to analyse the events surrounding important developments and issues that happened in this period. You need to understand how the different topics covered fit into the overall narrative. This book also explains the different types of exam questions you will need to answer, and includes advice and example answers to help you improve.

Features

As well as a clear, detailed explanation of the key knowledge you will need, you will also find a number of features in the book:

Key terms

Where you see a word followed by an asterisk, like this: Monopoly*, you will be able to find a Key terms box on that page that explains what the word means.

Key term

Monopoly*
Complete control – in this case, over trade with another country.

Activities

Every few pages, you'll find a box containing some activities designed to help check and embed knowledge and get you to really think about what you've studied. The activities start simple, but might get more challenging as you work through them.

Summaries and Checkpoints

At the end of each chunk of learning, the main points are summarised in a series of bullet points – great for embedding the core knowledge, and handy for revision.

Checkpoints help you to check and reflect on your learning. The Strengthen section helps you to consolidate knowledge and understanding, and check that you've grasped the basic ideas and skills. The Challenge questions push you to go beyond just understanding the information, and into evaluation and analysis of what you've studied.

Sources and Interpretations

Although source work and interpretations do not appear in Paper 2, you'll still find interesting contemporary material throughout the books, showing what people from the period said, thought or created, helping you to build your understanding of people in the past.

The book also includes extracts from the work of historians, showing how experts have interpreted the events you've been studying.

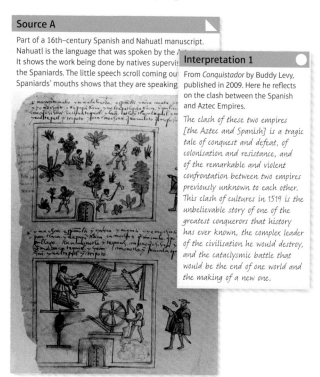

Source A

Part of a 16th-century Spanish and Nahuatl manuscript. Nahuatl is the language that was spoken by the A... It shows the work being done by natives supervis... the Spaniards. The little speech scroll coming out... Spaniards' mouths shows that they are speaking...

Interpretation 1

From *Conquistador* by Buddy Levy, published in 2009. Here he reflects on the clash between the Spanish and Aztec Empires.

The clash of these two empires [the Aztec and Spanish] is a tragic tale of conquest and defeat, of colonisation and resistance, and of the remarkable and violent confrontation between two empires previously unknown to each other. This clash of cultures in 1519 is the unbelievable story of one of the greatest conquerors that history has ever known, the complex leader of the civilisation he would destroy, and the cataclysmic battle that would be the end of one world and the making of a new one.

Extend your knowledge

These features contain useful additional information that adds depth to your knowledge, and to your answers. The information is closely related to the key issues in the unit, and questions are sometimes included, helping you to link the new details to the main content.

Extend your knowledge

The peasant colonisation scheme
Las Casas developed a scheme for setting up townships in which the natives would govern themselves; and, alongside this, a scheme encouraging peasants to leave Spain and work with the natives – showing them how to work the land as free people. Both these schemes failed. Spanish colonists opposed the township idea, and the natives were hostile to the Spanish peasants.

Exam-style questions and tips

The book also includes extra exam-style questions you can use to practise. These appear in the chapters and are accompanied by a tip to help you get started on an answer.

Exam-style question, Section A

Write a narrative account analysing the key events of 1527–33 that led to the fall of the Inca Empire.

You may use the following in your answer:

- the death of Huayna Capac (1527)
- the Battle of Cajamarca (1532).

You **must** also use information of your own.

8 marks

Exam tip

Plan your answer first by listing the main events that led to the fall of the Inca Empire. The question asks you to analyse the key events, so don't just describe them. Aim to make links between them. This will help you to structure your answer.

Recap pages

At the end of each chapter, you'll find a page designed to help you to consolidate and reflect on the chapter as a whole. Each recap page includes a recall quiz, ideal for quickly checking your knowledge or for revision. Recap pages also include activities designed to help you summarise and analyse what you've learned, and also reflect on how each chapter links to other parts of the unit.

THINKING HISTORICALLY

These activities are designed to help you develop a better understanding of how history is constructed, and are focused on the key areas of Evidence, Interpretations, Cause & Consequence and Change & Continuity. In the Period Depth Study, you will come across activities on Cause & Consequence, as this is a key focus for this unit.

The Thinking Historically approach has been developed in conjunction with Dr Arthur Chapman and the Institute of Education, UCL. It is based on research into the misconceptions that can hold students back in history.

  Cause and Consequence (3c&d) — conceptual map reference

The Thinking Historically conceptual map can be found at: www.pearsonschools.co.uk/thinkinghistoricallygcse

WRITING HISTORICALLY

At the end of most chapters is a spread dedicated to helping you improve your writing skills. These include simple techniques you can use in your writing to make your answers clearer, more precise and better focused on the question you're answering.

The Writing Historically approach is based on the *Grammar for Writing* pedagogy developed by a team at the University of Exeter and popular in many English departments. Each spread uses examples from the preceding chapter, so it's relevant to what you've just been studying.

Preparing for your exams

At the back of the book, you'll find a special section dedicated to explaining and exemplifying the new Edexcel GCSE History exams. Advice on the demands of this paper, written by Angela Leonard, helps you prepare for and approach the exam with confidence. Each question type is explained through annotated sample answers at two levels, showing clearly how answers can be improved.

Pearson Progression Scale: This icon indicates the Step that a sample answer has been graded at on the Pearson Progression Scale.

This book is also available as an online ActiveBook, which can be licensed for your whole institution.

There is also an ActiveLearn Digital Service available to support delivery of this book, featuring a front-of-class version of the book, lesson plans, worksheets, exam practise PowerPoints, assessments, notes on Thinking Historically and Writing Historically, and more.

ActiveLearn
Digital Service

Timeline: Spain and the New World

Columbus, Magellan and Pizarro

Columbus

Magellan

1492 Columbus' first voyage: lands on San Salvador
La Navidad built on Haiti

1493 Columbus' second voyage: governor of Haiti

1496 Bartholomew Columbus establishes Santo Domingo

1500 Columbus sent back to Spain in disgrace

1499 Francisco de Bobadilla replaces Columbus

1501 Gold mines on Haiti become productive

1502 *Encomienda* system set up in Haiti

1518 Smallpox epidemic in Haiti

1519 Magellan sets sail from Spain

1520 Magellan rounds Cape Horn into the Pacific Ocean

1521 Philippines: Magellan killed in battle with natives

1522 One of Magellan's ships returns to Seville: circumnavigation complete

1524 Pizarro's first expedition to Peru

1485	1490	1495	1500	1505	1510	1515	1520

1490 Spain united, religiously and politically

1494 Treaty of Tordesillas between Spain and Portugal

1503 *Casa de Contratacion*

1512 Laws of Burgos

1516 Death of King Ferdinand; Charles I becomes king

1518 Spanish government begins issuing *asientos*

1520 Gold and silver begin pouring into Spain via Seville

1524 Council of the Indies established in Spain

Balboa

Velázquez

Cortes

1510 Balboa founds Santa Maria de la Antigua del Darien

1511 Hatuey flees to Cuba, pursued by Velázquez

1513 Balboa claims Pacific Ocean for Spain

1514 Balboa arrested for treason and beheaded

1514 Conquest of Cuba complete

1519 Cortes lands in Mexico and claims land for Spain

1520 **May** Thousands of Aztec nobles massacred **June** Montezuma killed

1521 **Aug** Tenochtitlan falls and Aztecs surrender

The Spanish Empire

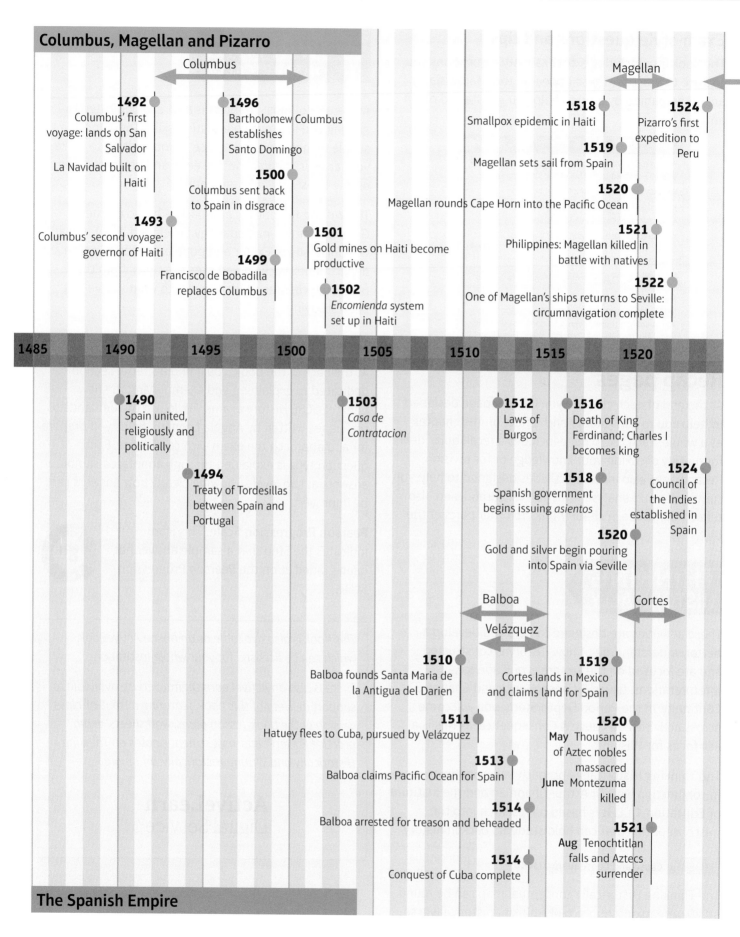

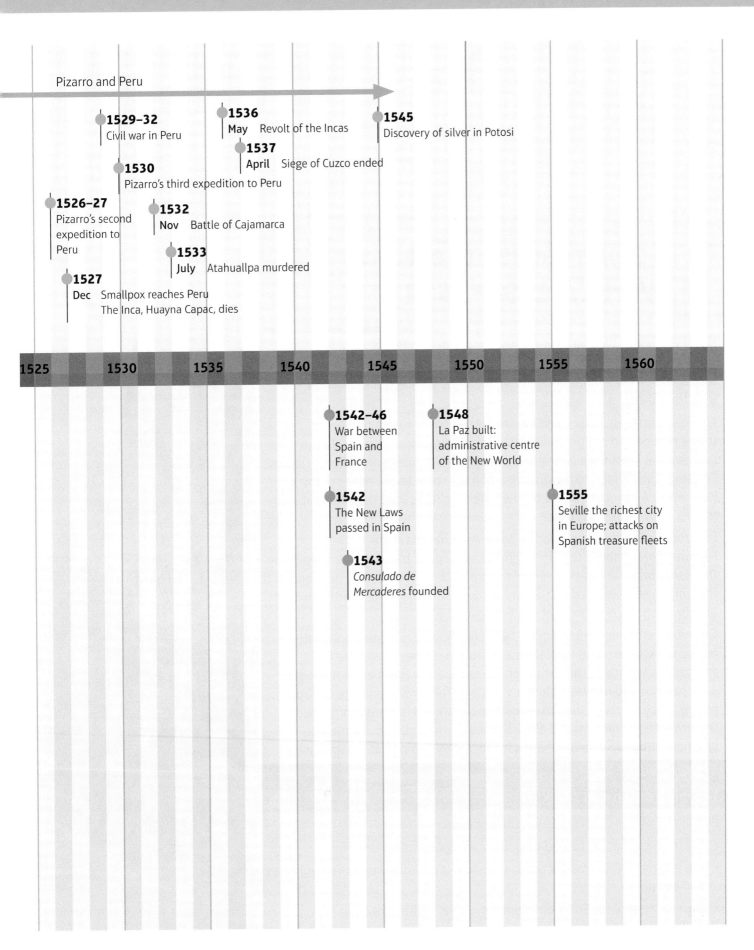

Pizarro and Peru

1529–32
Civil war in Peru

1536
May   Revolt of the Incas

1545
Discovery of silver in Potosi

1537
April   Siege of Cuzco ended

1530
Pizarro's third expedition to Peru

1526–27
Pizarro's second expedition to Peru

1532
Nov   Battle of Cajamarca

1533
July   Atahuallpa murdered

1527
Dec   Smallpox reaches Peru
The Inca, Huayna Capac, dies

1525	1530	1535	1540	1545	1550	1555	1560

1542–46
War between Spain and France

1548
La Paz built: administrative centre of the New World

1542
The New Laws passed in Spain

1555
Seville the richest city in Europe; attacks on Spanish treasure fleets

1543
Consulado de Mercaderes founded

01 | Spain reaches the 'New World', c1490–1512

Spain was politically united in 1479 under the joint rule of Queen Isabella of Castile and King Ferdinand of Aragon. By about 1490, it was religiously united too, as Isabella's religious enthusiasm led to the driving out of Muslims and Jews from the land.

A united, Christian Spain could look to Europe for its future prosperity through trade and political alliances – or it could look westwards. To the west lay the great Ocean Sea (the Atlantic Ocean), which no sailor had ever crossed. Crossing it could lead to the discovery of a sea route to the riches of the East Indies. A sea route would be much more reliable than the land route all traders used – but did it exist?

Christopher Columbus believed he could find that sea route. In 1491, Ferdinand and Isabella took the high-risk strategy of backing him. They did this partly because Isabella wanted to spread Christianity to any new lands that might be discovered on the way to the East Indies. It was partly, also, to out-do Spain's rival and neighbour, Portugal.

Columbus left Spain in September 1492 and, despite problems encountered on the voyage, he made landfall (reached land) six weeks later. He had reached the islands of the Caribbean. He returned to Spain in triumph, with gold, tobacco and natives. Columbus made further voyages to the Caribbean: he organised a colony; tried to encourage the spread of Christianity; made treaties with the natives; and almost wiped them out by unintentionally bringing European diseases – against which they had no natural immunity.

Learning outcomes

By the end of this chapter you will understand:

- the motives that lay behind Columbus' voyages of discovery
- the impact of Columbus' actions in the New World (the Americas, Caribbean and Bermuda)
- the significance for Spain of Columbus' claims in the Caribbean.

1.1 Spanish exploration

- Understand the importance of foreign ambition and religion in driving exploration.
- Understand why people were prepared to sponsor Columbus' plan to sail west, in order to discover a route to the east.
- Understand why Columbus' first voyage encountered difficulties, but was finally successful.

Spain c1490: exploration, religion and ambition

Most people in 1490 knew that the world was round. Astronomers, sailors, explorers and even the Catholic Church*, believed that this was so. Men drew maps based on this assumption, even though no one had yet sailed right round the globe. Most of Europe was known, measured and mapped. In order to chart more distant lands, map-makers used the information gained from navigators, travellers and merchants.

Key term

The Catholic Church*

In 1490, the Catholic Church, headed by the pope in Rome, was the only Christian Church in Europe.

Extend your knowledge

The Island of Atlantis

Throughout the 15th century, stories of discoveries of strange places and mythical creatures – some wildly improbable – circulated in the ports and harbours of Europe. The most persistent story concerned the Island of Atlantis. Many sailors claimed to have seen it, looming out of the mist, way out in the Atlantic Ocean. But no one had landed there. It was rumoured to be where seven Portuguese bishops and their followers had fled during troubled times, and where their descendants lived in peace and holiness. It was the dream of many sailors to find this island and its people, and reunite them with the Christian world.

Source A

This map of the world was drawn in about 1489 by Heinrich Hammer. He was a geographer and map-maker who lived and worked in Florence between 1480 and 1496.

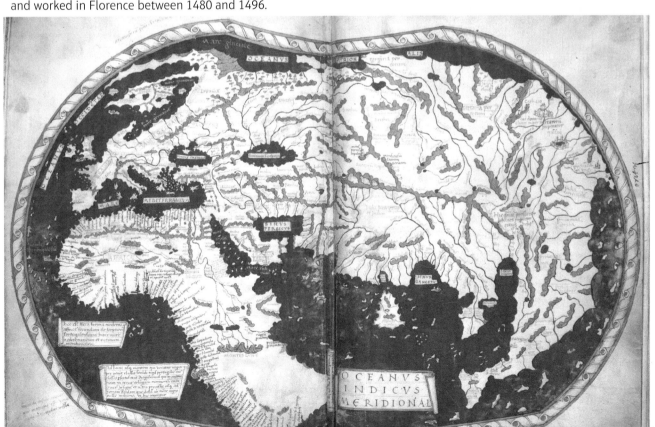

Foreign ambitions: east or west?

Towards the end of the 15th century, the ports of southern Europe must have been buzzing with excitement. Merchants and explorers returned with information about trade routes; claims about riches to be found; and stories about monsters to be defeated and dangers to be avoided. Uppermost in people's minds would have been the challenge of finding a sea route to the East Indies*. The spice trade* with those islands was well-established and extremely profitable. However, the overland route was becoming increasingly dangerous as attacks from bandits became more and more frequent. Could a safer sea route be found?

- The Portuguese had sailed south down the west coast of Africa and had almost reached the Cape of Good Hope. It was possible that, if this exploration continued, a sea route to the East Indies would be found by sailing east (See Figure 1.1).
- The Spanish had rediscovered the Canary Islands, and the Portuguese had discovered Madeira and the Azores, in the Atlantic Ocean. Maybe there was a chain of islands to be discovered, stretching across the Atlantic Ocean. Then, an island-hopping route could be found to the East Indies by travelling west.

There was a great deal to excite young men seeking adventure. The rewards would be high, but so were the risks. Ready to take risks, too, were the men with money. These were the bankers, wealthy merchants and agents of the European monarchs, who were always ready to back schemes that would make a profit. They would be trying to judge if there was a plan to find a sea route to the East Indies that was likely to succeed, and on which, therefore, it was worth them risking their money.

Key terms

The East Indies*

A term used to describe the lands and islands of south and south-east Asia. They are sometimes called the 'spice islands'.

The spice trade*

Trade between Asia and Europe in spices such as pepper, cardamom, ginger, turmeric and cinnamon.

The crusading spirit: spreading Christianity

Religion dominated the lives of people living in the 15th and 16th centuries. Christianity was the major religion in Europe. Christians were expected to go to church regularly and follow the rites and rules of the Catholic Church, led by the pope in Rome.

The Church was, however, more than just a religious organisation: it was also a political one. Monarchs going to war would ask for the blessing of the pope in order to justify their territorial invasions. They would claim to be fighting to defend the faith that they believed to be the only true one; though sometimes this was just an excuse to gain more land and power. Popes, too, encouraged and supported religious wars, and were frequently involved in the peace treaties that followed a war.

In the second half of the 15th century, the main concerns of the Catholic Church were:

- to defend Christendom* against outside threats
- to bring Christianity to any newly discovered countries – no matter what religion the people living there had previously held.

Many people believed that exploration and the discovery of new lands was part of a huge crusade* to spread Christianity throughout the world.

Key terms

Christendom*

The worldwide community of Christians. The eastern capital was Constantinople (modern Istanbul) and the western capital was Rome.

Crusade*

A crusade is a holy war.

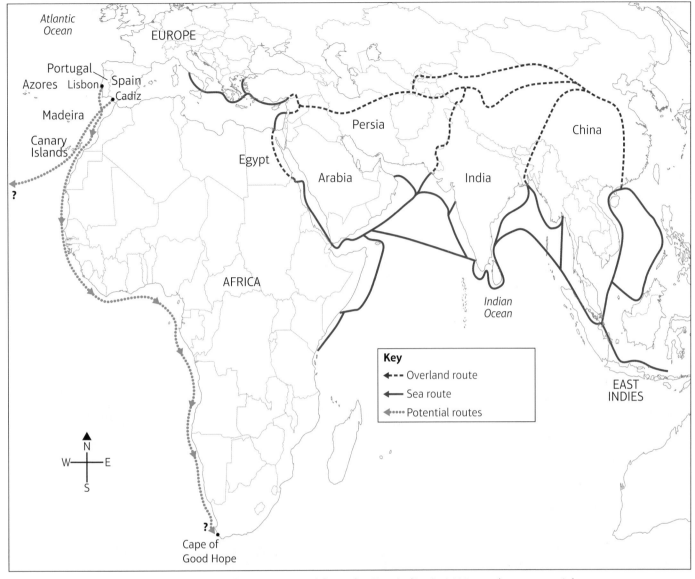

Figure 1.1 Map to show existing spice trade routes to and from the East Indies in 1491 – and two potential new ones.

Activities

1 Study Source A. This was probably the most up-to-date map available to explorers in 1490 who were trying to find a sea route to the East Indies. Work out with a partner:

 a how helpful this would have been

 b what problems this would have posed.

Remember not to use your 21st-century understanding of the world.

2 People with money would only finance the exploration of a sea route to the East Indies that was likely to be successful. Working in small groups, imagine you are bankers and must decide whether you are going to fund the exploration of a westwards, or an eastwards sea route to the East Indies. Remember to discuss the positive and negative aspects of each route. Which route did your group decide to support? Did other groups in your class reach the same decision?

3 Now write a report to your monarch, recommending one of the sea routes. Base your report on the discussions you had when you were working on Activity 2. Remember, that as well as saying why you support a particular route, you must also say why you cannot give your support to the other one.

Who was Christopher Columbus?
Columbus was born around 1451 in Genoa, Italy – the son of a weaver. Genoa was a busy port where merchants traded in all kinds of goods. As a young man, Columbus worked as a seaman on many different voyages, with different captains, in the Mediterranean and Aegean seas, and the coastal waters of the Atlantic Ocean. In 1476, the ship on which he was working was attacked and sunk. Columbus survived by clinging on to wreckage and swimming about 8km to the Portuguese shore. He made his way to Lisbon, where eventually he settled, married and had a son, who was born in around 1480.

Queen Isabella and King Ferdinand's refusal to support Columbus in 1486
A deeply religious woman, Isabella was determined to turn all non-Christians out of Spain. In 1486, she was involved in conquering Granada, a Muslim state in the south of Spain. She and Ferdinand had neither the time nor the money to support Columbus at that time.

Christopher Columbus: searching for a sponsor

In the 15th century, as now, large and expensive projects needed rich backers. These were people who could see the benefits of a particular project, believed in the abilities of the people who were leading it, and were prepared to risk money in sponsoring it. Setting up an expedition was extremely expensive: ships had to be bought or leased; navigational equipment installed; supplies bought and loaded; and crew members recruited and paid. This would be even more difficult – and therefore expensive – if the length of the voyage was uncertain because the exact geographical position of the destination was unknown.

People who were prepared to sponsor potentially risky projects usually had their own motives – which were not simply generosity. A wealthy merchant would see the advantage in finding a sea route to the East Indies: it would be more reliable than the current overland route and his profits would rise. European monarchs – always worried about the state of their treasuries – would be interested in sponsoring a voyage of exploration that could bring them wealth and status. It was to this last group that Columbus turned for sponsorship.

Timeline

Columbus searches for a sponsor for his 'Enterprise of the Indies'

1484 Approaches King John II of Portugal – sponsorship refused

1486–88 Sends representatives to King Charles VIII of France, and probably King Henry VII of England – sponsorship refused

1486 Approaches King Ferdinand and Queen Isabella of Spain – sponsorship refused

1491 Approaches King Ferdinand and Queen Isabella of Spain for the second time – sponsorship agreed

Why did Ferdinand and Isabella of Spain agree to sponsor Columbus?

Ferdinand and Isabella had religious and political reasons for agreeing to sponsor Columbus in 1491:

- Isabella's crusade to turn Spain into a completely Christian country had succeeded. By 1491, most Muslims and Jews had been forced out of Spain. Isabella was ready to continue crusading outside Spain, and was anxious to set up a great Christian mission in the East Indies.
- Isabella's personal priest and close friend, Juan Perez, was sympathetic to Columbus' enterprise, and provided him with lodgings and advice while he made his case to Isabella and Ferdinand.

- Spain would gain in international status if a Spanish-funded expedition found a sea route to the Indies before Portugal.
- A successful voyage would bring riches to the Spanish treasury and prosperity to Spain's merchants.

All these reasons combined to convince Ferdinand and Isabella that Spain should fund Columbus' expedition. It was agreed that Columbus would be given the title of 'Grand Admiral of the Ocean Sea', would be appointed governor of the newly colonised lands, and would have the right to one tenth of the produce of any new territories he discovered. Columbus' son later said that the terms were so generous because Ferdinand and Isabella didn't really expect his father to come back!

Source B

Columbus leaves Ferdinand and Isabella – by Theodor de Bry, 1594. The Spanish harbour of Cadiz can be seen in the background, and the royal Spanish coat of arms appears on the wall. Bry was an engraver, goldsmith, editor and publisher, famous for his illustrations of European expeditions to the Americas.

Activities

1 Imagine yourself as an adviser to Christopher Columbus.

   a What arguments would you have advised him to use when making his case for financial backing for his voyage of discovery? Write out the speech he might have made, remembering to stay in role for the 15th century.

   b Compare your arguments with those of another student. Are you making the same points? Whose argument is the more powerful? Why?

2 Look at the list of reasons why Ferdinand and Isabella decided to back Columbus. Put them in order of priority. Working with others in your group, produce an order with which you all agree.

THINKING HISTORICALLY — Cause and consequence (5b)

Relative importance

Historical events usually have many causes. Some are crucial, while some are less important. For some historical questions, it is important to understand exactly what role certain factors played in causing historical developments.

Significant factors in Ferdinand and Isabella's decision to sponsor Columbus' first voyage across the Atlantic Ocean in 1492

The importance of the spice trade between the East Indies and Europe.	Spain's treasury needing money by 1491.	Columbus was an experienced sailor anxious to prove that there was a westerly route to the East Indies.	Frequent attacks on merchants travelling the overland route between the East Indies and Europe.	Spain's desire for international importance.
Isabella's desire to set up a Christian mission in the East Indies.	Spain's merchants would prosper from a successful voyage.	Spain's need to dominate its rival, Portugal.	The refusal of John II of Portugal to sponsor Columbus in 1484.	Knowledge that the world was round.

1   Take an A3 sheet of paper. On the far right hand side, write 'Ferdinand and Isabella's sponsorship of Columbus'. Then write out each of the reasons in the above table onto a separate piece of card.

   a   Arrange all the reasons on the A3 sheet. On the right of the page, closest to where you have written 'Ferdinand and Isabella's sponsorship of Columbus', place the causes that happened immediately before their decision. Place the longer-term causes closer to the left of the page.

   b   Now draw lines between the reasons to show how they relate to each other: e.g. you could link 'Knowledge that the world was round' to 'Columbus was an experienced sailor anxious to prove that there was a westerly route to the East Indies'. Write along the link what the relationship is: e.g. 'Columbus knew that by sailing west he could arrive in the East Indies'. Make as many links as you can.

2   With a partner, draw up a table with four columns headed: 'Would have happened the same', 'Would have happened, but at a different time', 'Would have happened, but differently' and 'Would not have happened'.

   a   Consider the cause relating to Spain's treasury needing money. Would Ferdinand and Isabella have sponsored Columbus if their treasury had been full and the country not in need of money? Discuss as a pair what would have happened if that cause had not existed. Make sure you look at the other causes this cause is linked to. When you've decided, write the cause in one of your columns.

   b   Consider each of the other causes, discuss what would have happened without them, and write them into your table.

3   Using your diagram and your table, discuss with your partner which you think is the most important reason in explaining the timing of Ferdinand and Isabella's sponsorship. Working on your own, write a paragraph explaining which reason you think is the most important and why.

4   Does the cause you have chosen fully explain their decision? Add a second paragraph explaining why the other causes are still important.

Columbus' first voyage in 1492

Columbus' journal of his first voyage has been lost. However, it was seen, and extracts from it were copied by historian Bartolome de las Casas in the 1530s. He wrote the first biography of Columbus. Most of the information about Columbus' first voyage comes from these copies of Columbus' journal.

Finding the ships and crew

A royal decree required the Spanish port of Palos to provide Columbus with all the services he required. Two prominent citizens – the brothers Martin and Vicente Pinzon – worked with Columbus in finding and equipping the ships he needed. They agreed on hiring three sound ships: two caravels*, the *Nina* and the *Pinta,* and a carrack*, the *Santa Maria*, which Columbus used as his flagship.

Having found his ships, Columbus then set about looking for a crew. In this he was lucky. The Pinzon brothers, captains of the *Nina* and the *Pinta*, recruited most of the 80 or so men who were going to sail. Most of the men had experience of sailing to the Canaries. They were attracted, not only by the chance of adventure, but also by the promise of regular pay in an expedition that was backed by the Crown. As it happened, no one was paid until 1513 – but they didn't know that at the time. Additionally, Columbus hired Luis de Torres, who knew Arabic and Hebrew, to act as an interpreter in case they met natives whose language no one else understood. Preparing to sail too, were a handful of royal officials. There were neither soldiers nor any would-be settlers on board: this was a voyage of exploration and discovery. Unusually, for the time, there was no priest either.

Key terms

Caravel*

A small, fast, highly mobile sailing ship developed in the 15th century by the Portuguese to explore the African coast.

Carrack*

A three- or four-masted sailing ship developed in the 15th century by the Genoese, used mainly for commerce and for longer oceanic exploration.

Figure 1.2 This picture of the *Nina*, the *Pinta* and the *Santa Maria* was painted in 1882 by Francisco Pradilla Ortiz. He was a Spanish painter famous for creating historical scenes.

Equipping the ships

The ships were equipped with the usual supplies that would have been taken on exploratory voyages along the coast of Africa. There were bells, beads and necklaces for trading; and food – such as salted cod, pickled and salted meats, bacon and biscuits, flour and olive oil and dry pulses (e.g. chick peas, lentils and beans) – sufficient for feeding the crews for a year. There would also have been plenty of wine and barrels of fresh water. Columbus also took a number of blank pages: he was intending to keep a journal to record the voyage – something which was most unusual for the time.

Extend your knowledge

Navigation

Longitude, which tells sailors their east-west position, was unknown at the time of Columbus.

Latitude, which tells sailors their north-south position, was worked out in Columbus' time by measuring the angle of the sun at midday, using a quadrant.

Dead reckoning was used by sailors to work out their position, by calculating speed and distance from the starting point.

Setting sail

At 8 o'clock on the morning of 3 August 1492, the three ships slipped out of Palos harbour, heading for the Canaries – islands owned by Spain. They arrived six days later. There, repairs were made to the rudder of the *Pinta*, the *Nina*'s sails were re-rigged, and supplies of goats' cheese were taken on board. Finally, on 6 September, the three ships set sail into the unknown.

The journey had its problems:

- **Portuguese rivalry:** Shortly after setting out, Columbus had news from the captain of another ship that three Portuguese caravels were lurking in the eastern Atlantic, probably hoping to obstruct his voyage. Columbus made a slight adjustment to his route and so avoided them.

- **Sailors' fears:** Columbus realised that the sailors might become distressed the further they sailed from the Canaries without sighting land. On 10 September, after four days' sailing, he began keeping two sets of logs: in one, he recorded accurately the distance they had sailed – and this he kept secret; in the other, he recorded a shorter distance – so as not to frighten his crew.

- **Possible mutiny:** By 24 September, the crews became restless. None of the sailors had been out of sight of land for so long before. The crew seemed close to mutiny. The seriousness of the problem is described in Source C. Columbus persuaded the crews that they should carry on for another two weeks.

- **Quarrels about the route:** On 5 October, Columbus and Martin Pinzon quarrelled. Pinzon wanted the ships to make a sharp turn south, believing they would then be heading directly for Japan. Columbus, on the other hand, maintained that if they kept sailing straight ahead, they would reach China. Columbus won the argument.

Source C

Part of Columbus' journal – his daily record of the voyage.

September 24, 1492.

I am having serious troubles with the crew. All day long and all night long those who are awake and able to get together never cease to talk to each other in circles, complaining that they will never be able to return home. They have said that it is insanity and suicidal on their part to risk their lives following the madness of a foreigner. They have said that not only am I willing to risk my life just to become a great lord, but that I have deceived them to further my ambition. I am told by a few trusted men that if I persist in going forward they will throw me into the sea one night. I know that Martin [captain of the Pinta] cannot be trusted. He is a skilled mariner but wants the rewards and honours of this voyage for himself. I must use him for his support is too great amongst the men.

Unrest between Columbus, the captains and the crews, grumbled on. They had now been sailing for six weeks without sight of land. Finally, on 10 October – partly from a sense of desperation, and partly to encourage the crews – Columbus promised to give a silk coat to the first man who sighted land. That day, both Columbus and Martin Pinzon sighted land-based birds, and other sailors spotted a branch with berries floating in the sea. That night there was a full moon. A sailor on the *Pinta* suddenly shouted: 'land, land'. He had spotted a long, thin line of silver sand straight ahead.

The next day, Columbus, with the captains of the *Nina* and the *Pinta* and a hand-picked crew, rowed ashore. There, they raised the standard of Ferdinand and Isabella – a green cross, embroidered with the initials F and Y (for Ysabella) topped with crowns. In doing this, they claimed the land for Spain. But where were they?

Exam-style question, Section A

Write a narrative account analysing the key events of 1491–92 that led to Columbus sighting land in the New World in October 1492.

You may use the following in your answer:

- Queen Isabella and King Ferdinand's sponsorship
- preventing mutiny on the voyage.

You **must** also use information of your own.   **8 marks**

Exam tip

This question is testing your ability to pick out key events and explain why they were important. Don't just write down everything you know.

Summary

- Europeans needed to find a sea route to the spice islands of the East Indies.
- There was competition between Spain and Portugal to find it.
- It was known that the world was round, so sailing west to reach the East Indies could be sensible.
- Queen Isabella of Spain was very religious and she wanted to spread Christianity beyond Spain.
- King Ferdinand and Queen Isabella of Spain backed Christopher Columbus' voyage west.
- Columbus and his crews got safely to land on the other side of the Atlantic Ocean.

Checkpoint

Strengthen

S1 List the reasons why finding a sea route to the East Indies was important.

S2 Explain why Ferdinand and Isabella decided to sponsor Columbus' expedition.

S3 Describe the problems Columbus faced on his first voyage across the Atlantic Ocean.

Challenge

C1 Explain the importance of religion in the decision to sponsor Columbus' first journey.

C2 In your own words, summarise the three key reasons why Columbus was successful in making landfall in the New World.

If you are not confident about any of these questions, form a group with other students, discuss the answers and then record your conclusions. Your teacher can give you some hints.

1.2 Columbus reaches the New World

Columbus' actions in the Caribbean

Where, indeed, was Columbus? Figure 1.3 shows that he had reached what we now know to be the Caribbean islands. But that knowledge was in the future. At the time – and to his dying day – Columbus was sure he had reached the islands of the East Indies. Right from the start, Columbus was clear that he was on a voyage of exploration and discovery – not conquest. He spent the winter of 1492–93 exploring the Caribbean islands and looking, always, for gold and treasure.

San Salvador: the first contact with natives and gold

Columbus had raised the flag of Ferdinand and Isabella of Spain on the island he called San Salvador. He found out later that the natives called it Guanahani. Almost immediately on landing, Columbus and his men were met by a crowd of natives. In his journal, Columbus noted that they were completely naked; and some carried spears tipped with fish teeth and had marks of healed wounds on their bodies – but they seemed more curious than aggressive. Gifts were exchanged: hats, balls and glass beads from the Spanish; parrots, cotton and javelins from the natives.

It was on San Salvador that Columbus saw that the natives not only had painted faces, but they had gold ornaments hanging from small holes pierced in their noses. The natives told Columbus that their chief had a great deal of gold – even a ship made from it. This immediately sparked the interest of the Spaniards; but despite several days of friendly negotiations – made through sign language – Columbus could not persuade the natives to take him to their chief. They assured him, however, that gold was to be found further south.

Source A

This woodcut was made in about 1493, and is one of the earliest illustrations of Columbus and the natives of San Salvador.

Exploring the Bahamas and sailing to Cuba

Columbus believed that the natives on San Salvador were telling him the truth. On 14 October, he set off, looking for gold. Although he found several islands (the modern-day Bahamas) and captured a few natives to use as interpreters, Columbus failed to find gold. After time spent searching the small islands, he decided to head for a large island the natives had called Colba. This, he believed, would be Japan. He named the island Isla Juana in honour of Prince Juan, the son of Ferdinand and Isabella. That island was Cuba.

Building La Navidad

The captain of the *Pinta*, Martin Pinzon, was growing increasingly frustrated at having to follow Columbus' orders.

On 21 November 1492, the *Pinta* quietly slipped away without Columbus' permission. Martin Pinzon was looking for gold on his own. This was to have serious consequences.

This act of rebellion left Columbus with two ships: the *Nina*, commanded by Martin's brother, Vicente; and Columbus' flagship, the *Santa Maria*, which he commanded. On Christmas Eve 1492, the *Santa Maria* ran aground. It was completely stuck on a coral reef off the north coast of Haiti. In a letter to Ferdinand and Isabella, Columbus reported that he was asleep at the time, and blamed a boy who was steering the ship; later, he was to blame poor ship-building. Columbus later decided that the hand of God was behind the shipwreck. Wherever the fault lay, something had to be done in a hurry.

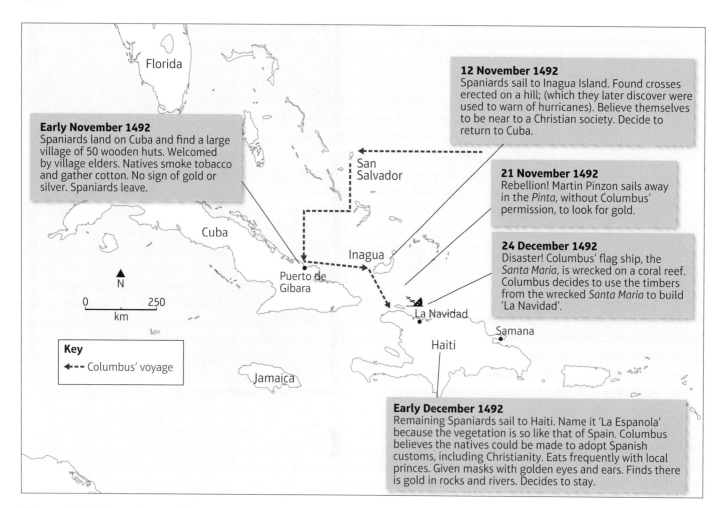

Figure 1.3 Sailing in the Caribbean: decisions and disasters.

The local chief, Guacanagari, sent natives to help the Spaniards unload all the goods and equipment from the doomed ship. This was done quickly, but the shipwreck left Columbus with a dreadful dilemma.

The *Pinta* had vanished and the *Santa Maria* was wrecked: Columbus had only one usable ship and this was the smallest – the *Nina*. There was no way in which all his men could be carried back to Spain in one small ship. Some had to be left behind on Haiti. It had never been Columbus' intention to occupy territory in the New World, but now he had no choice. Using timbers from the wrecked *Santa Maria*, the Spaniards built some huts surrounded by a moat, and with a look-out tower in case of trouble. Thirty-nine men stayed behind, including a doctor and an interpreter. Their job was to collect samples of gold and wait for the next Spanish expedition to arrive.

Extend your knowledge

La Navidad
La Navidad is Spanish for Christmas. Columbus gave the settlement this name because it was founded on Christmas Day.

Activities ?

1 What conclusions could Columbus and his men have drawn from what they saw and heard when they landed on San Salvador? Work with a partner and compare your conclusions with others in your class. Remember to back up your conclusions with evidence.

2 Look at Figure 1.3. At each point, Columbus had to make a decision, and each decision had an outcome. In groups, reflect on the decisions he made. Were they the correct ones? In what ways might the consequences have been different if he had made a different decision? Compare your conclusions with those reached by others in your class.

3 Working in groups of three or four, create a conversation between Columbus and a group of Spaniards – some of whom want to stay in Navidad, and some desperate to get back to Spain. What arguments will they use? How will Columbus reply?

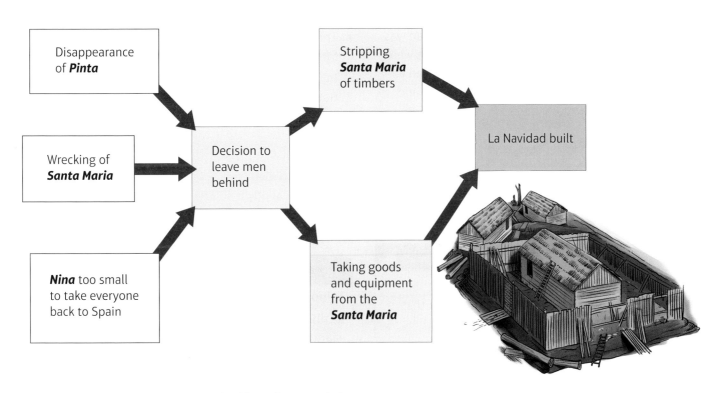

Figure 1.4 Key events leading to the building of La Navidad.

The impact of contact with the 'Indians'

The natives who met Columbus and his crew on San Salvador were clearly friendly. Natives and Spaniards exchanged gifts, and there was no evidence of any hostility between them. However, as the Spaniards landed on more islands and made contact with different groups of natives, it became clear that their exploration was driven by their desire to find gold. This led to growing hostility and treachery on both sides.

Gold, cotton and tobacco

Columbus and his crew saw that the natives on San Salvador (see page 19) were wearing beautiful gold jewellery. The natives would not tell the Spaniards where the gold had come from. Because of this, the Spaniards were only able to find small amounts of gold in the river sands and rocks on Haiti. Martin Pinzon, captain of the *Nina*, left the expedition (see page 20) to look for gold – following up a rumour that it was plentiful on a nearby island. When he rejoined the expedition, he had enough gold to convince Ferdinand and Isabella that there was more to be found.

On Cuba, the Spaniards noted that the natives gathered 'cotton' from trees. Columbus noted in his journal that he saw strong ropes, blankets and hammocks made from cotton on Haiti. What the Spaniards had seen was not, in fact, cotton. We now know that the natives were gathering kapock from ceiba trees*. Kapock looked very like cotton and could be spun into strong thread and woven into cloth.

Columbus described, in his journal, first seeing natives smoking herbs on Cuba and inhaling the smoke. It became clear that some regularly smoked tobacco in the form of cigars. Spaniards sailing with Columbus quickly picked up the habit.

> **Key term**
>
> **Ceiba trees***
>
> Trees that produced light, fluffy balls of kapok that could be spun into thread or woven into cloth.

Relations with the Tainos and Caribs

The Tainos* people were the natives usually encountered by Columbus:

- Those living on San Salvador were a branch of the Tainos, and were both curious and friendly when they met the Spaniards (see page 19).
- On Cuba, in November 1492, the Spaniards came across a large village consisting of about 50 wooden huts, thatched with palm leaves. This was a Tainos settlement, and they greeted Columbus and his men peacefully.
- A Tainos chief sent his men to help off-load goods and equipment from the wrecked *Santa Maria* and gave Columbus permission to build La Navidad on his land.
- Columbus noted that the Tainos were so peaceful that they would make good slaves, and so gentle and kind that they could easily be converted to Christianity.
- The Tainos believed that the Spaniards were 'men from the sky' whose arrival fulfilled the prophecies of their elders. This may well account for their initial acceptance, and even excitement, at the arrival of the Europeans.

It was a different matter with the Caribs*:

- They lived mainly on the Caribbean islands of Guadalupe and Martinique (east of the Bahamas).
- They were constantly raiding the Tainos, mainly to steal women and girls.
- There were rumours amongst the Tainos, and later the Spaniards, that the Caribs were cannibals.
- In Columbus' journal, he tended to describe all natives who were armed as 'Caribs' and those who were not as 'Tainos'. This led to some confusion as to which natives were actually involved in the incident at Samana (see opposite).
- Columbus also recorded the first case of violence between Spanish and natives in the New World. He referred to them as 'Caribs', but later translations said they were 'Tainos'.

> **Key terms**
>
> **Tainos***
>
> A tribe of native people living on the Caribbean islands, who were usually peaceful.
>
> **Caribs***
>
> A tribe of native people living on the Caribbean islands, who were usually war-like, and possibly cannibals.

Source B

An illustration from the first Latin edition of Columbus' Letter on the First Voyage, published in about 1530. It shows the native Indians as cannibals.

An incident at Samana

On its way back to Spain, the *Nina* was forced to anchor off Samana, in Haiti, because of bad weather, and some of the crew members went ashore. They found a settlement hung about with dried human heads, and canoes large enough for 150 men. The arrival of heavily painted natives – armed with bows and arrows tipped with fish bones and painted with poison – should have further alarmed them. Maybe the natives thought the Spaniards were looking for slaves or gold – and maybe that was what the Spaniards really were doing.

One warrior met Columbus on board the *Nina* and assured him that there was plenty of gold on the island. Columbus rewarded the native with food, pieces of green and red cloth and beads. The man was sent ashore, together with crew members, with orders to return with gold. As they landed on the shore, armed natives emerged from the trees, ready to attack. Columbus' men offered to buy the bows and arrows but, after they had bought two, the atmosphere turned nasty. The natives attacked and the Spaniards retaliated, wounding at least two of them. The natives fled and the whole frightening episode ended.

The incident had shown that the natives – whether Tainos or Caribs – were prepared to attack the Spaniards. Columbus recorded in his journal that the Indians would have to learn to fear the Christians. Here, stories of cannibalism amongst some native peoples began to circulate, and the Spanish linked these to the Caribs.

Source C

Part of a letter written by Columbus to Luis de Santángel in 1493, announcing his discoveries.
Luis de Santángel was Ferdinand's finance minister.

As for monsters, I have not found a trace of them except at the point in the second isle as one enters the Indies, which is inhabited by a people considered in all the isles as most ferocious, who eat human flesh. They possess many canoes, with which they overrun all the isles of India, stealing and seizing all they can. They are not worse looking than the others, except that they wear their hair long like women. They are ferocious compared to these other races, who are extremely cowardly; but I only hear this from the others.

Activities ?

1 Make a list of the outcomes of the contact between Spaniards and natives. Put them in order of importance (a) at the time and (b) for the future.

2 'An incident at Samana' was written from the point of view of the Spaniards because it was based on what Columbus wrote in his journal. Rewrite the incident from the point of view of one of the natives.

3 Write a short paragraph to explain how likely you think it was that there was cannibalism on the islands that Columbus explored on his first voyage. Remember to back up what you say with evidence.

Columbus' return to Spain

Despite fierce storms, Columbus reached Lisbon, in Portugal, on 4 March 1493 and he reached the Spanish port of Palos on 15 March. Ferdinand and Isabella were not, initially, worried that Columbus had made landfall in Portugal – this was, however, to cause trouble later. They sent him letters of congratulation, addressing him by all the titles they had agreed should be given to him if his enterprise was successful, and urging him to meet with them in Barcelona as soon as he could. Columbus made his way back to Barcelona, cheered by crowds as he went. He was the hero of the hour!

Interpretation 1

From Laurence Bergreen, *Columbus The Four Voyages 1492–1504*, published in 2011.

The sudden, unauthorised construction of a manned fort [La Navidad] served Columbus's interests first and foremost. Until he hit upon this scheme, he had agreed to a single voyage. Now he would have to return in the name of Spain, if only to relieve the crew, who had become hostages to his ambition, marooned off the coast of Haiti, unable to return home until he fetched them. Only Columbus and a few of his officers and pilots knew where in the world this fortress was located, and only they would be able to find it again.

Figure 1.5 This picture of Ferdinand and Isabella receiving Christopher Columbus was painted by the French artist Joseph Nicolas Robert-Fleury, in 1846.

The role of the pope

One of the factors that persuaded Isabella to sponsor Columbus had been her crusading spirit: she was determined that the Spanish would spread Christianity in any newly discovered lands. Ferdinand and Isabella therefore enlisted the support of the pope for their claim to the 'Spanish Indies'. In this they were lucky: Spanish himself, Pope Alexander VI was excited by the news of Columbus' discoveries and determined that Christianity would be spread to these newly discovered lands.

The impact of rivalry with Portugal

The first European monarch that Columbus met on his return from the New World was King John of Portugal. As a result of what he learned, John believed Portugal had a rightful claim to the lands Columbus had discovered. Immediately, he sent a Portuguese chief magistrate to meet with Ferdinand and Isabella. They, too, were hoping to open up negotiations with Portugal. They sent a representative to the Portuguese capital, Lisbon, to set up a meeting. Meanwhile, he was to make it clear that no ship would be allowed to sail to the New World without their permission, and that there should be no Portuguese activities in any of the lands discovered by Columbus.

Source D

From part of Pope Alexander VI's declaration of support for Ferdinand and Isabella's claim to the lands Columbus had discovered. It comes from the document *Inter Caetera*, issued by the pope in May 1493.

Our dear son Columbus, not without great labour, danger and expense, ensured that, with ships and men suitable for the task, he sought remote and unknown lands across seas where no one previously had sailed.

In consequence of which, you have decided to submit to us [spiritually] the said lands and the islands and their inhabitants and to convert them with the help of divine charity to the catholic faith.

Just as some kings of Portugal discovered, and acquired, the regions of Africa and other islands, so we concede to you and your heirs and successors the islands and lands discovered by you, with the same rights, privileges and liberties.

Ferdinand and Isabella were busy encouraging Columbus to plan a second voyage to the Indies. They confirmed all his titles; issued him with a new coat of arms and awarded him a pension for life, in recognition of him having been the first to discover the new lands across the seas. Additionally, they gave him powers enabling him to govern lands in the New World, but under the overall authority of the Spanish crown. Ferdinand and Isabella were preparing to settle and establish a government in the lands discovered by Columbus. Portuguese officials and royal advisers were worried. Which country had rights to what, needed to be sorted out – and quickly.

The Treaty of Tordesillas, 1494

On 7 June 1494, agreement was reached between Spain and Portugal. An imaginary line was drawn from the North to the South Pole, about 2,000km to the west of the Cape Verde islands. All lands to the west of the line would be Spanish; to the east of the line, with the exception of the Canary Islands, all lands would be Portuguese.

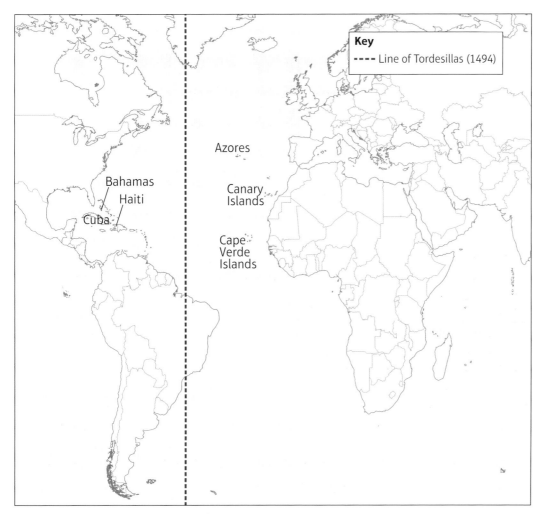

Figure 1.6 A map to show the Line of Tordesillas (1494) and the New World Columbus discovered on this first voyage.

Activities ?

1 Work in small groups with an even number of students in each group.

   a Half your group should make a case for Portugal having control of exploration in the New World; the other half should make a case for Spain having control.

   b Each group should then put its case to the class. Whose argument do you find the most persuasive? Why?

2 The Treaty of Tordesillas (1494) was supposed to settle the differences between Spain and Portugal. Reading about the Treaty and looking at Figure 1.6, what problems do you think it might have created?

Exam-style question, Section A

Explain **two** consequences of Christopher Columbus' return to Spain in March 1493.   **8 marks**

Exam tip

Don't rush into writing an answer. Think about different types of consequences, and consequences for whom? What were the consequences for Columbus? For Spain? For Portugal? Were there short-term consequences and long-term consequences?

Summary

- Columbus discovered San Salvador, Cuba and Haiti.
- The native Tainos were usually peace-loving, but the Caribs were often war-like.
- Columbus' flagship, the *Santa Maria*, was shipwrecked off the coast of Haiti.
- Columbus arrived back in Spain to great celebrations.
- Columbus' discoveries intensified Spanish-Portuguese rivalry.

Checkpoint

Strengthen

S1 Give examples of relations between the Spaniards and the natives.

S2 Describe what happened to the wrecked *Santa Maria*.

S3 Explain why Columbus' discoveries intensified Spanish-Portuguese rivalry.

Challenge

C1 Explain why Columbus believed he had landed in the islands of the East Indies.

C2 Look back at what Ferdinand and Isabella hoped to gain from Columbus' voyage. How much, in their eyes, had he achieved?

C3 In your own words, summarise the reasons why the pope got involved in Columbus' discoveries.

How confident do you feel about your answers to these questions? If you're not sure you answered them well, work in groups of three, with each person focusing on one of the challenge tasks. Then report your answers back to the group.

Was Columbus a good governor?

It was clear, from the titles given to Columbus, that Ferdinand and Isabella expected him to set up and govern settlements in the New World. He was not expected to open up new trade routes or conquer new lands. For his second expedition, they supplied him with a fleet of 17 ships. These ships carried around 1,200 people: priests, gentlemen, farmers and skilled craft workers. They also carried animals, seeds and agricultural tools. But Columbus was primarily an explorer. Was he able to, and did he really want to, take on the role of governor?

La Navidad and Isabela

On 28 November 1493, the second expedition reached La Navidad (see page 20) and found it burned to the ground. Columbus was told by a local chief that the Spaniards had begun stealing native women for sex, as well as hunting for gold. Some Tainos had attacked the Spaniards and, in the fighting, all the Spaniards had been killed and La Navidad destroyed.

Columbus found a site for a new settlement and named the city that was built there 'Isabela' in honour of Queen Isabella. However, the city never prospered. This was partly due to the site, but mainly due to the Spanish settlers. They were adventurous and greedy – more intent on finding gold than clearing forests and planting crops. Columbus then decided to leave his role as 'governor' to others. Thinking of himself as 'Admiral of the Sea', he took off to explore the southern coastline of Cuba. His journal records that, in the summer of 1494, he intended to return to Haiti, but the winds were blowing in the wrong direction. He set sail anyway and, in July 1494, he landed on Jamaica. The natives there welcomed the Spaniards with food that was better than any they had had elsewhere, and gifts were exchanged. Columbus finally got back to Haiti in September 1494.

Source A

The title page of a history of Spain and the New World c1601, by chronicler Antonio de Herrera y Tordesillas. It shows an engraving of La Navidad before and after its destruction.

27

Santo Domingo

Early in 1496, Columbus returned to Spain. He wanted to report progress; and he wanted to deal with complaints that had been made to the monarchs about the way he was running Isabela. While he was away, Columbus left his brother Bartholomew in charge of Isabela. Bartholomew immediately began building a new settlement, Santo Domingo, on a site on the south coast of Haiti. The site was promising: it was by the mouth of the Ozama river, that was teeming with fish and provided a natural harbour. The soil appeared to be fertile as there were plenty of palms and fruit trees growing wild. A new settlement was built quickly and all the inhabitants of Isabela were moved there.

In 1498, Columbus returned to Haiti and found Santo Domingo in uproar. The Tainos, irritated by constant demands for food and women, were on the point of refusing to co-operate with the Spaniards. Many of the Spaniards, disillusioned and hungry, were in open revolt against Bartholomew's authority. Columbus managed to restore order by:

- pardoning the Spanish rebels
- giving each of the rebels a parcel of land
- providing native labourers to work this land.

Columbus' disgrace

Although Columbus' actions calmed the situation for a time, the damage had been done. Rebellion after rebellion broke out and, eventually, Columbus was forced to take a stronger line. Spaniards and Indians were hanged, and Indians' homes destroyed, as Columbus struggled to keep order. Exhausted and ill, he sent two ships back to Spain carrying messages asking the Cortes* to appoint a royal commissioner to help him govern.

However, reports of trouble in the Caribbean had already reached Ferdinand and Isabella. In the spring of 1499, the Cortes appointed Francisco de Bobadilla to take over from Columbus and to investigate complaints against him. Arriving in Haiti in September 1500, Bobadilla upheld all the complaints, had Columbus arrested and sent him back to Spain in chains.

Ferdinand and Isabella agreed that Columbus should keep his titles, but that these would be in name only. They said that never again could he actually work as admiral or viceroy – and he most certainly could not interfere in the government of the Indies.

Key term

Cortes*

The Spanish parliament, consisting mainly of nobles and wealthy middle-class men. Under Ferdinand and Isabella, it mainly approved the monarchs' decisions, but it kept a tight control over taxation.

Activities ?

1   Work in small groups. Draw a 3×3 table, with three vertical columns headed: 'La Navidad', 'Isabela' and 'Santo Domingo'; and three horizontal rows labelled: 'What were the problems?', 'What did Columbus do to resolve them?' and 'What happened as a result?' The table could be drawn on a large flip chart. Use the information in this section to complete the table.

2   How might Columbus have defended his actions? How might Bobadilla have made out a case against him? Working in pairs – one of you taking Columbus' side and the other Bobadilla's – find at least three points to make on each side.

3   Do you agree that Ferdinand and Isabella were right to say that Columbus should never again be involved in governing the Indies? Write a paragraph to explain your thinking, remembering to support what you say with examples.

What were the effects of Spanish settlement for the native Indians?

The discovery of inhabited lands, on the other side of the Atlantic Ocean, presented a marvellous opportunity to Ferdinand and Isabella. They could develop their crusading spirit (see page 10) by bringing Christianity to previously unknown lands, while at the same time extending Spain's power and influence in the world. However, this raised the problem of what to do with the people who were already living in 'Spain's' New World'. How were the natives to be treated? What was the impact on them – both intended and unintended – of the arrival of the Spanish?

Gold and tribute

On his first voyage, Columbus had failed to find the vast supplies of gold he had promised Ferdinand and Isabella. He was determined to put this right on his second expedition. In 1495, he focused on the centre of Haiti: destroying the native population living there, and setting up a chain of forts. The native population were forced to pay tribute to the Spaniards. This was usually paid in cotton or vegetables; but when it was paid in gold, extreme efforts were made to find out where the gold came from. Clearly there were gold mines on the island, but Columbus was not able to exploit them fully before he was disgraced.

One of Bobadilla's first actions as governor was to develop gold mining in the centre of Haiti. He allowed any Spaniard to go and try their hand at mining. The only requirement was that they paid an eleventh of what they found to the Crown. This had an immediate effect – and 300kg of gold was found in 1501 alone. But it was the natives who did most of the hard physical work.

Under the governorship of Ovando, who succeeded Bobadilla (see page 28), gold mining flourished, with the natives providing the workforce in conditions close to slavery. Mining and washing for gold became organised, and official places for the melting of gold were built. After initial set-backs – caused largely by the Spaniards' lack of understanding of both mining techniques and how to manage the Indian workforce – Haiti gradually became the treasure house Columbus had predicted.

But this had been achieved at tremendous cost to the natives. Tainos and Carib societies had been destroyed and the people were forced to provide slave labour for the Spanish invaders.

Source B

An engraving by Theodor de Bry, made in 1596, showing Indians mining gold in Haiti. Bry was an engraver, goldsmith, editor and publisher. He was famous for his illustrations of European expeditions to the Americas.

Slaves and slavery

Columbus had despaired of finding sufficient gold to satisfy his sponsors. He therefore decided to try to compensate for this by sending slaves back to Spain. There was nothing unusual in this: slaves were valuable goods and were bought and sold in the main markets of Spain.

- Columbus master-minded a series of armed expeditions into every part of Haiti with the aim of kidnapping as many native Indians as possible.

- These armed campaigns were cruel, bloody and violent. The Spaniards didn't distinguish between Tainos and Carib: all they wanted was captives who could be shipped back to Spain and sold as slaves.

- The Indians fought back, but were no match for the Spaniards; thousands of Indians fled to the mountains and the Spanish called this a 'rebellion'.

Columbus had failed to realise that Ferdinand and Isabella had not yet decided what their policy was going to be regarding slaves and slavery in the Caribbean. On 24 February 1495, a ship left Isabela, loaded up with about 550 natives to be shipped back to Spain. About 200 died on the journey, and over half were ill when they finally arrived in Cadiz. Isabella was horrified. She had some trained as interpreters, some were used to row her ships, while others were released and sent back to Haiti. Although African slaves were frequently bought and sold in Spanish markets, Isabella was shocked at the thought of natives from the New World being treated in the same way. One of her aims in sponsoring Columbus had been to spread Christianity. She wanted the natives of the New World to become Christians – not slaves.

Timeline

1495 550 natives shipped back to Spain as slaves

1502 Nicolas de Ovando becomes Governor of the Indies

1503 Suppression of native revolt by Spaniards, including the Jaragua massacre; first *encomiendas* granted to conquistadors and Spanish officials

The encomienda system

It was the *encomienda** system that turned the Indians into slaves on Haiti. This happened under the governorship of Nicolas de Ovando, who replaced Francisco de Bobadilla in 1502. When Ovando landed on Haiti, the natives were in revolt against the Spaniards. Ovando and his men ruthlessly supressed the rebellion, and then set up a system of government intended to prevent anything like that happening again. Central to this was the *encomienda* system. Under this system, each Spaniard, called an *encomendero**, was assigned a set number of natives. The natives had to provide 'tribute' to the Spaniards; this could be in the form of labour, or goods, or both. In return, the Spaniards would provide protection from warring tribes and would teach the natives the Spanish language and about Christianity.

Key terms

Encomienda*

The system whereby Spanish settlers protected the native Indians in return for tributes.

Encomendero*

The name given to a man in charge of an *encomienda*.

Source C

From *A Short Account of the Destruction of the Indies* written by Bartolome de las Casas in 1542. He was a Dominican priest (see page 33) and one of the first settlers in the Indies. He gave up his *encomienda* and his Indian slaves in 1515. Later, he worked as a bishop in Mexico and was appointed 'Protector of the Indians'.

The Spaniards learned – even the labourers and those who came on a salary to dig and work the land and extract the gold from the mines – to loaf around and walk proudly, eating from the sweat of the Indians and seizing each by force, three, four and ten to serve them, because of the gentleness of the Indians, who neither could, nor knew how, to resist.

Smallpox

In 15th-century Europe, diseases such as smallpox*, measles and influenza were killers. The Tainos and Caribs had no natural resistance to these diseases, and hundreds died from them in the years after the Spaniards arrived – unknowingly carrying these diseases with them. In the winter of 1518, for example, a terrible epidemic of smallpox swept through the islands.

It has been estimated that there were around 500,000 Indians living on Haiti when Columbus landed there in 1492. By 1507, when the Spanish took a census, they found only 60,000 remained. The Spanish had slaughtered thousands of Indians; and thousands more had died from disease or from being kept as slaves in terrible conditions.

Key term

Smallpox*

An infectious disease caused by a virus. The symptoms are a rash that develops into blisters in the mouth and on the skin. It can cause blindness and death. Those who survived generally had pock-marked skin. Smallpox was declared eradicated from the world in 1980.

1 Work in groups.

   a Make a list of all the factors that brought about change in the relationship between Indians and Spaniards.

   b On a large sheet of paper, turn each factor into a spider diagram. Along each 'leg' of the spider, write the effects that factor had on the natives. Are any of the 'legs', from different spiders, the same? Join them up if they are.

2 Looking at your 'spiders', which one had the greatest effect on the natives? When you have decided, choose one person (or, if your group is large, two people) to make out a case for that factor being the most important in bringing about change. Make your presentation to the rest of the class. At the end of the presentations, all the class should vote on which factor they think is the most important.

3 Write a paragraph to explain how the search for gold changed the relationship between Spaniards and Indians.

Spain develops an imperial policy* toward the Caribbean

Ferdinand and Isabella sponsored Christopher Columbus in order to find a route to the East Indies. In doing so, it was expected that this route would greatly benefit Spain and bring riches to the Spanish treasury. It was also hoped that Columbus' expedition would lead to the spread of Christianity beyond Europe. What no one anticipated was that Columbus would discover lands that had never before been seen by Europeans, and that Spanish people would want to settle there. A policy had to be drawn up that would control development in this 'New World'.

Key term

Imperial policy*

The policy developed by the Spanish government towards its growing empire in the New World.

The regulation of further exploration

Columbus was not the only person sailing west in the years after his first voyage. There were also independent explorers who, attracted by the promise of adventure and treasure, set sail across the Atlantic. Ferdinand and Isabella needed to establish Spanish control over exploration and discovery in the New World.

On 10 April 1495, Ferdinand and Isabella issued a decree that imposed strict conditions on anyone sailing to the New World:

1 Every ship setting off for the Caribbean, whether for exploration or settlement, had to leave from the Spanish port of Cadiz and had to be registered with the authorities there.

2 Anyone wanting to live in the Indies could do so freely. If they discovered gold, they could keep one third of what they found: the remaining two thirds had to go to the Spanish Crown. One tenth of all other products had to be sent back to Spain.

3 One tenth of the cargo carried by ships sailing to the New World had to be Spanish.

The establishment of a monopoly* on trade

In 1503, Isabella set up the *Casa de Contratacion* (House of Trade) as a government agency working in Spain's southern capital, Seville. What did it do?

The work of the *Casa de Contratacion* was intended to make sure that all trade with the Caribbean was controlled by Spain, and that all profits from that trade came into the Spanish treasury. In reality, there was a lot of smuggling as people tried to get around the rules and regulations. Nevertheless, the aim of the Spanish monarchs was clear: Spain had to control access to the New World.

Key term

Monopoly*

Complete control – in this case, over trade with another country.

Figure 1.7 The work of the *Casa de Contratacion*.

The seven callout bubbles read:
- Collect all taxes levied on goods entering Spain.
- Collect all taxes levied in the Indies.
- Approve all voyages of exploration and trade.
- Licence captains and train prospective navigators.
- Collect and keep up-to-date, secret information on trade routes and discoveries.
- Make sure that all trade with the Indies is carried in Spanish ships.

The extension of Spanish authority

Ferdinand and Isabella had to make sure that Spanish rule extended to, and was maintained, in the New World. It was essential that this was done if Spain was to profit from the discovery of the Caribbean islands, and if Christianity was to be spread amongst the natives.

The importance of Santo Domingo

Shortly after the arrival, in 1502, of Nicolas de Ovando as governor, a tremendous hurricane destroyed most of the town. This was Ovando's opportunity to rebuild the town as a centre of Spanish administration and the capital of Haiti.

- There were to be wide roads and squares surrounded by imposing stone buildings.
- These buildings were designed to house administrative offices where, for example: rules and regulations were issued, taxes and tributes were collected, and contact with Spain was maintained.
- Spanish courts were set up so that Spanish justice could be administered.

- There was to be a governor's house, a hospital, houses for merchants and bankers and a great new cathedral.

By 1512, most of the building work was complete. All traces of Christopher and Bartholomew Columbus had gone. Santo Domingo was officially the capital city of Haiti and the headquarters for the exploration and conquest of the New World.

Source D

A modern photograph of the cathedral of Santa Maria La Menor in Santo Domingo. It was built between 1512 and 1540.

The role of Catholic missionaries

One of the motives behind Ferdinand and Isabella's sponsorship of Columbus' first voyage was their desire to spread Christianity beyond Europe. When Ovando set sail from Spain in 1502, he had with him 17 Franciscans* and four priests. The Franciscans were to set up their Order in Haiti and the priests were to preach, and help convert and baptise the Indians. These were the first Christian missionaries in the New World.

In 1503, Ferdinand and Isabella issued a series of rules for the education of Indians into a 'civilised' Christian life:

- Indians were to live in towns under a Spanish protector and pay taxes.
- They would be taught about Christianity and baptised into the Christian faith, and would be expected to give up their non-Christian beliefs.
- They would also be taught to read and write, and how to dress 'decently'.

It was quite clear what the missionaries had to do.

Reports reached Spain about the abuse of Indians on Haiti. These horrified the Archbishop of Seville, who was a senior churchman, and he sent a group of Dominican* missionaries to Haiti to try to stop the mistreatment. On 4 December 1511, a packed cathedral listened in shock as the Dominican Antonio de Montesinos denounced them for their treatment of the Indians – accusing them of cruelty and tyranny.

Key terms

Franciscan*

A member of a Roman Catholic religious community (monk) seeking to persuade people to become Christians by example – by living a life of poverty and humility, as Christ had done.

Dominican*

A member of a Roman Catholic religious community (monk) seeking to persuade people to become Christians by teaching and preaching about Christ.

The Laws of Burgos: December 1512

The Laws of Burgos were introduced as the result of recommendations made to Ferdinand by a committee of religious and academic leaders.

These laws:

- upheld the *encomienda* system (see page 30), where Indians worked for a Spanish *encomendero* and were paid a salary for the work they did
- called for Spanish officials to be established in every town to punish any Indian who broke the laws
- laid down detailed regulations regarding Indians' hours of work, housing, clothing and feeding, and insisted they were treated kindly
- laid down detailed instructions as to how the Indians were to be instructed in Christianity.

Although the law-makers accepted the principle that all Indians were free, they decided that most Indians were not capable of making use of that liberty. Some concessions were made to the chiefs, who were excused from basic jobs and allowed servants. Generally, however, Indians were to come under the care and protection of the Spanish. The price they had to pay for this 'protection' was the abandonment of their traditional way of life and conversion to Christianity.

Activities ?

1 How would a Spanish official have explained why Spain wanted to control exploration in the New World? Write a report to Ferdinand, explaining why this had to be done.

2 Imagine you are a 16th-century smuggler, anxious to trade with Haiti. With a partner, work out how you would you get around the rules laid down by the *Casa de Contratacion*. Analyse the risks you would be taking.

3 Work with a partner and read through the Laws of Burgos (1512). One of you must make out a case for the laws being good for the Spaniards. The other must make out a case for the laws harming the natives. Argue with each other – who has the best argument?

Exam-style question, Section A

Explain **two** of the following:

- the importance of Santo Domingo for Spanish control of the New World
- the importance of a monopoly of trade for Spanish control of the New World
- the significance of Roman Catholic missionaries for the development of the New World in the years to 1512.

16 marks

Exam tip

This question targets your ability to explain the importance of a specific development. Don't be tempted to describe it: focus on its importance. A good answer will provide specific detail in support of its importance.

Summary

- La Navidad and Isabela failed as settlements, but Santo Domingo flourished.
- Complaints about the cruel and arrogant way Columbus governed Haiti led to his arrest and disgrace.
- The *encomienda* system turned the Indians into slaves, making them work for the Spanish and pay tribute to them.
- Compulsory conversion to Christianity was part of the *encomienda* system.
- Some Catholic missionaries tried to make the lives of the Indians more tolerable and their efforts were shown in the 1512 Laws of Burgos.
- The Spanish brought European diseases to Haiti, against which the Indians had no immunity.
- Spanish officials tried to control voyages to, and trade with, the Caribbean.
- Santo Domingo became the administrative capital of Haiti and the headquarters for the exploration and further conquest of the New World.

Checkpoint

Strengthen

S1 Describe three ways in which Columbus' governing of Haiti could be criticised.

S2 How did the *encomienda* system benefit Spain and the Spanish settlers? Give three examples.

S3 How did Christianity change the lives of the Indians on Haiti? Give three examples.

Challenge

C1 How reasonable was it for Ferdinand and Isabella to expect Columbus to be a good governor? Explain your answer.

C2 Create a flow chart showing the stages by which Spanish attitudes to the Indians changed from Columbus' first encounter with them to the Laws of Burgos in 1512.

If you are not confident about any of these questions, form a group with other students, discuss the answers and then record your conclusions. Your teacher can give you some hints.

Recap: Spain reaches the 'New World', c1490–1512

Recall quiz

1 When did Columbus set out on his first voyage?

2 Which monarchs sponsored Columbus?

3 Name the three ships that sailed on Columbus' first voyage.

4 What was the aim of Columbus' first voyage?

5 Who were the Tainos?

6 What did the Treaty of Tordesillas (1494) agree?

7 Who replaced Columbus as governor of Haiti?

8 What was the name of the organisation, set up in Spain in 1503, that controlled contact between Europeans and the Caribbean?

9 Name the missionary who preached in Santo Domingo against slavery.

10 What was the date of the Laws of Burgos?

Activities ?

1 Copy and complete the table below. It aims to match expectations with what actually happened.

What did they expect?	What did they get?
By sailing west, Columbus expected to find…	The first landfall Columbus made was…
King Ferdinand and Queen Isabella expected great wealth…	Columbus brought back…
The native Indians expected the Spanish…	By 1512, the native Indians had…
Spanish settlers expected to find gold very easily…	Gold was found… but…
Christian missionaries expected to convert…	By 1512, they had…

2 a Draw up a table in which you note the changes that happened to the Indians on Haiti. Use these three headings: 'Changes to ways of living', 'Changes to ways of working' and 'Changes in relationships with others'.

b What do you think drove these changes and why? Write a paragraph in explanation.

3 Explain how the Spanish brought Haiti under their control.

Names and Places ?

Match the following names and places to their definitions below:

Christopher Columbus	Third governor of Haiti
Francisco de Bobadilla	A native tribe generally thought to be war-like
Martin and Vicente Pinzon	Native name for the island of Cuba
Nicolas de Ovando	First explorer to reach the New World
Antonio de Montesinos	A native tribe generally believed to be peaceful
Caribs	Captains of the *Pinta* and *Nina* respectively
Tainos	The first Caribbean island reached by Columbus
Colba	Second governor of Haiti
San Salvador	Dominican priest who preached against Spanish treatment of natives
Cadiz	Settlement on Haiti founded by Bartholomew Columbus
Isabela	Spanish port used by Columbus
Santo Domingo	Settlement on Haiti founded by Christopher Columbus

Writing historically: building information

When you are asked to write an explanation or analysis, you need to provide as much detailed information as possible.

Learning outcomes

By the end of this lesson, you will understand how to:

- add clear and detailed information to your writing by using relative clauses and noun phrases in apposition.

Definitions

Relative clause: a clause that adds information or modifies a noun, linked with a relative pronoun, e.g. 'who', 'that', 'which', 'where', 'whose'.

Noun phrase in apposition: two noun phrases, positioned side-by-side, the second adding information to the first, e.g. [1] 'Seville, [2] the centre for New World trade, became the wealthiest city in Europe.'

How can I add detail to my writing?

Look at a sentence from the response below to this exam-style question:

> Explain the importance of the settlement at La Navidad (1492) for Spanish exploration of the New World. **(8 marks)**

> The settlement at La Navidad, which was built from the wrecked 'Santa Maria', showed the Spaniards' intention to stay and explore the New World further.

The main clause is highlighted in yellow. The relative pronoun is highlighted in green. The relative clause is highlighted in purple.

This noun phrase is modified by this **relative clause**: it provides more information about La Navidad.

1. How could you restructure the sentence above using two separate sentences?

2. Why do you think the writer chose to structure these sentences using a main clause and a relative clause instead of writing them as two separate sentences?

Now look at these four sentences taken from the same response:

> Only the 'Nina' was left to sail back to Spain. It was not large enough to take all the sailors home. Columbus desired to return to explore further. A rescue mission gave him just cause.

3. How effectively is this information expressed? Write a sentence or two explaining your answer.

4. How could you improve the written expression in the answer above, using relative pronouns?

   a. Rewrite the sentences, using relative pronouns to link all the information in **one** sentence.

   b. Now rewrite the sentence using relative pronouns to link the information in **two** sentences.

   c. Which version do you prefer? Is the information most clearly and fluently expressed in one, two or four sentences? Write a sentence or two explaining your choice.

How can I add detail to my writing in different ways?

You can also add detail to a sentence using a **noun phrase in apposition**.

Compare these sentences:

> *The burning of La Navidad, which was the first European settlement in the New World, showed the resentment building up amongst some of the natives.*

This uses a relative clause to add information clearly and briefly.

> *The burning of La Navidad, the first European settlement in the New World, showed the resentment building up amongst some of the natives.*

This uses a noun phrase in apposition to add the same information even more clearly and briefly.

5. How could you combine the information in the pairs of sentences below using a noun phrase in apposition?

> *La Navidad's population was an important justification for a second expedition. They were in need of rescue.*

> *Columbus returned to find La Navidad destroyed. La Navidad had been a symbol of co-operation between the Spaniards and the natives.*

Did you notice?

6. If you remove the relative clause or the noun phrase in apposition from the two sentences at the top of the page, they both still make sense. They are also both separated from the rest of the sentence with commas. Can you explain why? Write a sentence or two explaining your ideas.

Improving an answer

Look at the extract below from another response to the exam-style question on the previous page:

> *La Navidad was one of the reasons for Columbus' second expedition. He had to rescue the Spaniards he had left behind. The king and queen could not abandon their subjects. Columbus reached La Navidad in November 1493. He found it burnt to the ground and all the Spaniards had been killed. This was the start of the hatred between the Spaniards and the natives of the New World.*

7. a. Rewrite the information in the answer above, making it as clear and brief as possible. You could use:

- relative clauses

- nouns in apposition.

b. Look carefully at your response to Question 7a. Are all your sentences easy to read and understand, or are some of them too long and confusing? If so, try rewriting them to make their meaning as clear as possible.

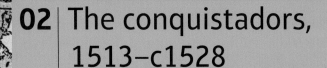

02 | The conquistadors, 1513–c1528

By 1513, it was generally accepted in Europe that an unknown continent had been found by Columbus, and that it was a barrier between Europe and Asia.

It was Spain and the conquistadors who were to show that, although this new continent was a barrier, it was also to bring riches beyond most people's wildest imaginings. The conquistadors were armed adventurers and explorers, who set out west, looking for gold, glory and power. Each man hoping to be a conquistador had to finance his own expedition and find like-minded adventurers to join him. The Spanish monarchs were involved in supporting the conquistadors, and would sometimes invest in a particular conquistador's venture. Monarchs gave the conquistadors the right to invade and conquer in the name of Spain, and allowed some the right to become governors of specific regions of the New World.

The conquistadors were expected to send regular reports back to Spain and to act on orders sent to them by Spanish administrators; but they didn't always do this. Sometimes, time, distance and the speed with which events moved in the New World prevented this happening and sometimes, conquistadors simply chose not to obey orders, preferring to act independently. Conquistadors also had to give the monarch one fifth of all gold and treasure they found. In these ways, the monarchs not only hoped to enrich the Spanish treasury, but also to control how the Spanish empire was growing.

This control, however, was very limited; partly because instructions from Spain took such a long time to arrive in the New World, but mainly because of the native population. The conquistadors were not claiming empty lands: the New World was inhabited by natives, many of whom were part of civilisations far older than that of Spain. Though this did not seem to trouble the invading Spaniards much: massacre, murder, treachery, enslavement, rape and torture marked the conquistadors' blood-soaked exploration of the New World.

Learning outcomes

By the end of this chapter, you will understand:

- the importance of the conquistadors in the expansion of the Spanish Empire
- the significance of establishing settlements on mainland America
- the reasons why the Spanish Empire expanded so rapidly.

2.1 The start of an empire

Spain begins to build an empire in the west

Columbus had shown that there were lands across the Atlantic Ocean, and treasure to be found. Conquistadors*, small-time adventurers and potential settlers followed in his footsteps and branched out on explorations of their own, claiming new territories for Spain. In this way Spain built its empire in the west.

Timeline

Balboa the conquistador

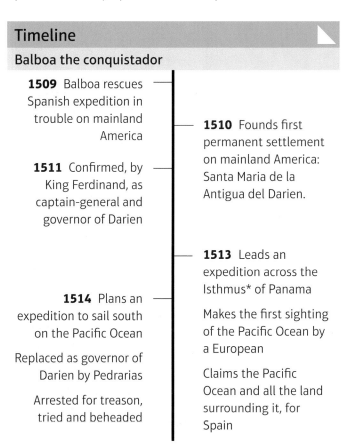

1509 Balboa rescues Spanish expedition in trouble on mainland America

1510 Founds first permanent settlement on mainland America: Santa Maria de la Antigua del Darien.

1511 Confirmed, by King Ferdinand, as captain-general and governor of Darien

1513 Leads an expedition across the Isthmus* of Panama

Makes the first sighting of the Pacific Ocean by a European

Claims the Pacific Ocean and all the land surrounding it, for Spain

1514 Plans an expedition to sail south on the Pacific Ocean

Replaced as governor of Darien by Pedrarias

Arrested for treason, tried and beheaded

Key terms

Conquistador*

An armed adventurer and explorer who went to the New World looking for gold, glory and power.

Isthmus*

A narrow strip of land, with sea on both sides.

Rescuing an expedition

Vasco Nunez de Balboa was a Spanish explorer and conquistador. In 1509, he led a party that rescued a Spanish expedition from mainland America. The group had been almost wiped out by sickness and hostile natives. They were waiting with their leader, Francisco Pizarro, either for help, or for death at the hands of the natives.

Balboa found the ill-fated expedition. Together with other Spanish settlers, he drove the natives out of the region of Darien (see Figure 2.2) where the soil was fertile and a settlement likely to be successful.

Establishing a settlement

Under Balboa's leadership, the abandoned Indian village in Darien quickly became a Spanish settlement called Santa Maria de la Antigua del Darien. It was the first European settlement on the American mainland, and was to be the starting point of the Spanish take-over of Central America. The settlement flourished because Balboa:

- made the Spaniards build houses and plant crops
- dominated the natives with a combination of force and friendship
- collected vast quantities of food and gold from the natives.

The whole area of Darien became so prosperous and important in Spanish colonial trade that, by 1513, it was being called *Castilla de Oro*, which means 'Golden Castile', in recognition of the prosperity Darien brought to Spain, and in particular to Castile.

Exploration, treasure and conquest

Balboa, confirmed as a captain general and governor of Darien by Ferdinand in 1511, had a free hand to do more or less as he pleased when invading and conquering in the name of Spain. This included torturing the natives (see Source A).

Source A

Balboa and the conquistadors used many different ways to torture the natives. One way was using fighting dogs. This is a 16th century engraving by Theodor de Bry, who was a Belgian engraver known for his pictures of explorers. It shows Balboa ordering homosexual natives to be killed by dogs. De Bry never visited America but his work was based on eyewitness accounts.

Balboa and the rest of the conquistadors were driven on, not just by their desire for treasure, but by rumours of a vast sea in the west, bordered by fabulous kingdoms rich in gold. The rumours turned out to be true. On 1 September 1513, Balboa set out on a journey across the Isthmus of Panama (see Figure 2.2). His expedition consisted of 190 Spaniards, some native guides and a pack of dogs. One of the men with him was Pizarro, who later discovered Peru (see Chapter 3).

After weeks of exploration, the excited explorers sighted a great, shimmering ocean from a densely wooded mountainside. They were the first Europeans to set eyes on what they called the 'Southern Sea' and which the explorer Ferdinand Magellan (see page 46) was later to name the Pacific Ocean. Scrambling down to the shore, Balboa strode into the sea and claimed it, and the lands surrounding it, for Spain.

Trekked westward, exploring interior of central America.

Claimed land for Spain as they explored.

Spanish gunfire and fighting dogs killed and injured hundreds of natives.

Took with him 190 Spaniards, 1,000 natives and a pack of fighting dogs.

Many gold objects given by natives to appease war-like Spanish.

Much gold stolen from natives in battle.

Figure 2.1 Balboa explores Central America, 1513.

Balboa, with 80 men and some natives, began exploring the coast in canoes made from tree-trunks. A local chief gave them baskets full of pearls as gifts, and before long they found more pearls themselves. They took hundreds away with them and some were sent back to Spain.

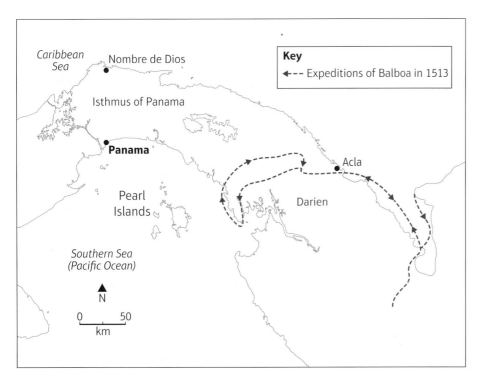

Figure 2.2 A map showing the expeditions of Balboa in 1513.

Opening the path to empire

Balboa's exploration had opened up long-term possibilities for Spanish expansion into the New World.

- By revealing the existence of the Southern Sea, and claiming it and the lands surrounding it for Spain, he had provided the motivation for further Spanish exploration and conquest of previously unknown territories.

- His exploration of the Isthmus of Panama had shown how narrow the strip of land separating the two oceans was, and so encouraged those who were still searching for a westward sea route to the east.

- He had shown, by sending large quantities of treasure – mainly gold and pearls – back to Spain, that any further exploration was likely to be hugely profitable.

Exam-style question, Section A

Explain **two** consequences of Balboa's exploration of the Isthmus of Panama.　　　　　**8 marks**

Exam tip

The question is asking you about consequence. Make sure you focus your answer on what happened as a result of Balboa's exploration of the Isthmus of Panama, and not on what led up to it.

Pedrarias and Espinosa: exploring the 'south seas'

Pedrarias was a Spanish official. In 1514, appointed by the king, he sailed to Darien to take over as governor from Balboa. Balboa had been informed that he was to be replaced, but the hand-over did not go well. Pedrarias and Balboa were old enemies. Balboa was waiting on the Pacific coast, with 300 men and four ships. Balboa told Pedrarias he was planning to sail south and explore the lands there.

Pedrarias, though, was suspicious. He thought Balboa was planning to stop him becoming governor. Because of this, Pedrarias had Balboa arrested and charged with treason. One of the men sent to arrest Balboa was the conquistador Pizarro, who had been with him when the Pacific Ocean was discovered, and whom Balboa had rescued from a failed expedition in 1509. At the end of his trial in the town of Acla, Balboa was condemned to death. He was beheaded, and his head was left in the town square for several days as a warning to others. Pedrarias and Espinosa, his second in command, were now free to explore the Southern Sea.

The significance of Panama

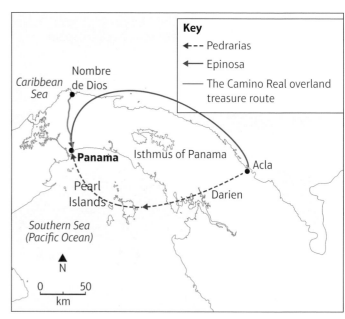

Figure 2.3 A map showing the expeditions of Pedrarias and Espinosa after 1514.

Pedrarias and Espinosa explored separately (see Figure 2.3), but ended up at the same point on the Pacific Ocean, which they agreed would be a good place for a settlement. This settlement was in Panama. It was the closest in distance to Nombre de Dios, on the Caribbean coast, making communication with Spain as easy as possible. This settlement was significant because:

- it was situated on the Pacific Ocean, closest in distance to Nombre de Dios on the Caribbean Sea
- a route (the Camino Real) between Panama and Nombre de Dios was the quickest way of moving goods, treasure, messages and people between the Pacific Ocean and the Caribbean Sea
- the land surrounding Panama was fertile and had sea teeming with fish
- Panama was a port, well-situated for Spanish treasure ships to off-load their cargoes.

By 1522, most of the inhabitants of Darien (the settlement created by Balboa) had been forcibly removed to Panama by the Spanish. The few, mainly Spaniards, who remained were massacred by the natives, and the buildings set on fire. The first European settlement on the mainland had been destroyed.

Setting a pattern

As they explored, searching for gold and claiming land for Spain, the conquistadors allied with the local chiefs and tribes. However, after these alliances, the Spanish sometimes destroyed the local villages. The burning of villages, the killing of natives and the destruction of their way of life, became the pattern of all future Spanish expeditions into mainland America.

Figure 2.4 The pattern of empire building by the Spanish conquistadors.

Activities ?

1 Imagine you are a conquistador wanting to recruit young men to come with you to explore and conquer in the New World. Design a poster that will attract them to join you on your next adventure. Use the information in this section to decide what qualities you will be looking for.

2 Working in groups:

 a draw a table with two columns: head one 'Balboa' and the other 'Pedrarias and Espinosa' – list their achievements

 b now think about the part the three men played in setting the foundations of the Spanish Empire in the New World and put them in order of importance. Compare your group's order with that of other groups in your class and arrive at an order with which you all agree.

3 Reflect on the ways in which these conquistadors treated the natives and the pattern of conquest that was developing. Discuss with a partner whether or not this was likely to create trouble for the Spanish Empire as it grew in the New World. Keep a note of your conclusions so that you can check later whether or not you were correct.

Velázquez conquers Cuba

Timeline

The conquest of Cuba

1511 Hatuey, a native chief living in Haiti, flees to Cuba with 400 natives to escape Spanish cruelty

Velázquez and 300 conquistadors pursue them

1512 After strong native resistance, Hatuey is captured and burned alive

1513 Massacre at Caonao – thousands of natives killed

1514 Conquest of Cuba complete

City of Santiago de Cuba founded and becomes capital of Cuba

1515 City of Havana founded

Velázquez was one of the men who went with Columbus on his second voyage to Haiti (see page 27) and he was never to return to Europe. He helped Columbus subdue the rebels in Santo Domingo, and ended up as deputy governor in charge of the west part of Haiti.

Source B

A 16th century engraving by Theodor de Bry, the Belgian engraver. It shows the death of Hatuey as he is burned at the stake by the invading Spaniards. De Bry never visited America but based his engravings on eyewitness accounts.

It was in around 1511, that the following events combined to lead to the invasion of Cuba:

- Death from illness, and at the hands of the Spanish, had reduced the number of natives on Haiti who could be used as slaves, and more were needed to work as labourers for the Spaniards.

- Many natives, desperate to escape the cruelty of the Spaniards, had fled to neighbouring islands. One of them, a chief called Hatuey, escaped to Cuba in 1511, with as many of his surviving people as he could (this totalled around 400 people). One of Hatuey's aims was to warn the Cuban natives about the brutality of the invading Europeans.

Extend your knowledge

Hernan Cortes

Hernan Cortes travelled with Velázquez to Cuba. He was responsible for making sure that the right amount of treasure was returned to Spain. Later, when Velázquez became Governor of Cuba, Cortes worked as his secretary. In 1518 – by which time he was extremely rich – he led an expedition to Mexico and wiped out the Aztec civilisation.

Hatuey's fate

Velázquez and over 300 conquistadors set off in pursuit of Hatuey. Hatuey led a fierce native resistance against Velázquez; but, being an escaped slave, the Spanish could not let Hatuey win. They wanted to make an example of him, to stop other natives resisting in the future. It took Velázquez three months to corner and capture Hatuey.

A captured enemy leader had to be put to death, and the only question was how this should be done. Hatuey was offered death by execution if he converted to Christianity by being baptised. Hatuey is supposed to have said that if becoming a Christian meant spending eternity with the Spaniards, he would prefer not to convert. Because of this, the Spaniards tied him to a stake and burned him alive (see Source B).

The conquest of the island of Cuba then began. It was not difficult. The island, though bigger than Haiti, was mainly forested and contained fewer people. Initially, the Spanish strategy was to approach a village, send the priest and historian Bartolome de las Casas to persuade the natives to supply the Spaniards with food, and negotiate with them to hand over half of their village to the invaders. This usually worked – but at Caonao things went badly wrong.

Massacre at Caonao, 1513

Caonao, in Cuba, was a large town, with two squares surrounded by houses. About 2,000 natives gathered to watch the Spanish enter the town and still more watched from their houses. Food was prepared and given to the invaders, who then demanded entry to the largest house. When the natives refused to grant the Spanish entry, one Spanish soldier went wild and began killing the natives. More Spaniards started to join in, and Spanish soldiers forced their way into the house and began slaughtering all the natives they could find.

The massacre at Caonao marked a turning point in the invasion of Cuba.

- Any resistance on the part of the natives was met with immediate violence.
- The priest, Bartolome de las Casas, turned against Spanish policies and spent the rest of his life working for good treatment of the natives.

Establishing a colony

By January 1514, the conquest of Cuba was complete and the Spanish could establish themselves wherever they wanted on the island. Velázquez was responsible for founding several towns, the most important of which were Santiago de Cuba, the capital, founded in 1514, and Havana, founded in 1515.

Source C

From Bartolome de las Casas' *A Short Account of the Destruction of the Indies* published in 1542. He was a priest and historian who travelled with Velázquez to Cuba and stayed there for several months. Here, he describes the impact of the massacre at Caonao.

Once all the inhabitants of this island [Cuba] found themselves in the same hopeless predicament as those on Hispaniola [Haiti] – that is, they were either enslaved or foully murdered – some began to flee into the hills while others were in such despair that they took their own lives. Men and women hanged themselves and even strung up their own children. As a direct result of the barbarity of one Spaniard (a man I know personally) more than two hundred locals committed suicide, countless thousands in all dying in this way.

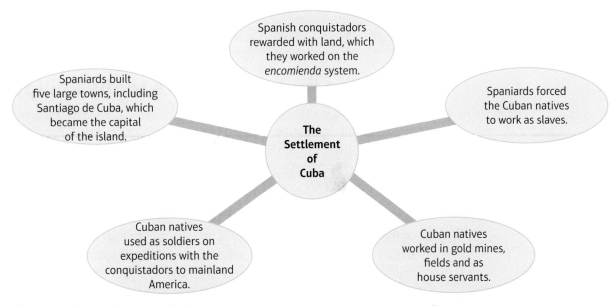

Figure 2.5 The settlement of Cuba.

Exam-style question, Section A

Write a narrative account analysing the key events of 1511–14 that led to the conquest of Cuba.

You may use the following in your answer:

- the death of Hatuey (1512)
- the massacre at Caonao (1513).

You **must** also use information of your own.   **8 marks**

Exam tip

The question targets your ability to write an analytical narrative. It is important that you don't just describe what happened, but that you explain the connections between the events that led to the conquest of Cuba.

The massacre of thousands of natives during the Spanish conquest was followed by more native deaths from malnutrition, disease, overwork and suicide. The native population of Cuba fell, from 350,000 in 1514, to little more than 3,000 by 1555. Meanwhile, the Spaniards prospered.

Source D

From Bartolome de las Casas *A Short Account of the Destruction of the Indies* published in 1542. Las Casas was a priest and historian who travelled with Velázquez to Cuba and stayed there for several months.

There was one royal official who, when he was allotted 300 natives, worked them so hard that, at the end of three months, only thirty were still alive, the other two hundred and seventy having perished down the mines. Later, he received another consignment of much the same number, and he saw them off, too. The more he received, the more he killed, until eventually he himself died and the Devil took his soul.

During the three or four months I was there, more than seven thousand children died of hunger after their parents had been shipped off to the mines, and I saw many other horrors, too.

Activities

1   Work in pairs. One of you write an account of the conquest of Cuba from the point of view of a conquistador; the other write about the conquest from the point of view of a Cuban native. You must not use more than 150 words each.

2   Compare the points you have made with the pair working next to you. What are the differences and what are the similarities in the accounts you have written?

3   Now work as a whole class. Can you identify any common themes running through the accounts written from the point of view of a conquistador, and those written from the point of view of a Cuban native?

Magellan finds a sea route to the Philippines

Columbus had wanted to find a route to the spice islands of the East Indies by sailing west. He failed. Instead, he discovered the islands of the Caribbean. Even though Spain was building an empire in the Caribbean, and the Pacific Ocean had been claimed for Spain, a sea route to the spice islands had still not been found.

In March 1518, the new king, Charles I of Spain, put Ferdinand Magellan in command of a fleet of five ships. Charles thought that it wasn't clear, from the Treaty of Tordesillas (see page 25), whether the spice islands belonged to Spain or Portugal. It seemed to Charles that if a Spanish explorer could find a way to those islands by sailing west across the Atlantic Ocean, the spice islands would belong to Spain. Magellan, an excellent navigator, wanted the challenge of finding out whether or not this mysterious sea route really existed.

On 20 September 1519, Magellan sailed away from Spain with his five ships: the *Trinidad, San Antonio, Santiago, Concepcion* and *Victoria*. The ships were heavily armed, and carried 270 men and enough food and water to last for a year.

Magellan and his ships managed to circumnavigate* the world between 1519 and 1522 and claim the Philippines for Spain. This was important because:

- it meant that Spain could claim the spice islands – as they had found a western route to it
- it brought prestige to Spain – Magellan and his ships were the first to complete a voyage of global circumnavigation.

However, this came at a cost.

> **Key term**
>
> **Circumnavigate***
> To travel (usually sail) around the world.

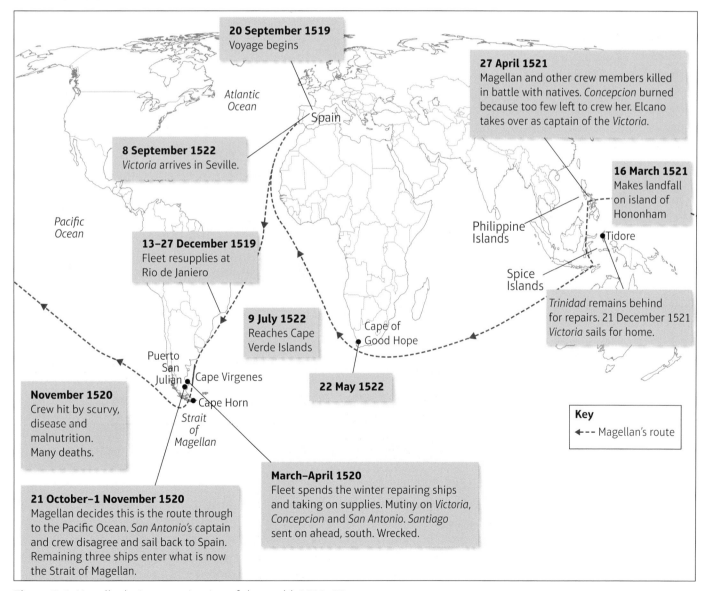

20 September 1519
Voyage begins

27 April 1521
Magellan and other crew members killed in battle with natives. *Concepcion* burned because too few left to crew her. Elcano takes over as captain of the *Victoria*.

Atlantic Ocean

Spain

8 September 1522
Victoria arrives in Seville.

16 March 1521
Makes landfall on island of Hononham

Pacific Ocean

Philippine Islands

Tidore

13–27 December 1519
Fleet resupplies at Rio de Janiero

Spice Islands

Trinidad remains behind for repairs. 21 December 1521 *Victoria* sails for home.

9 July 1522
Reaches Cape Verde Islands

Cape of Good Hope

Puerto San Julian

Cape Virgenes

22 May 1522

November 1520
Crew hit by scurvy, disease and malnutrition. Many deaths.

Cape Horn

Strait of Magellan

Key
◄--- Magellan's route

21 October–1 November 1520
Magellan decides this is the route through to the Pacific Ocean. *San Antonio's* captain and crew disagree and sail back to Spain. Remaining three ships enter what is now the Strait of Magellan.

March–April 1520
Fleet spends the winter repairing ships and taking on supplies. Mutiny on *Victoria, Concepcion* and *San Antonio. Santiago* sent on ahead, south. Wrecked.

Figure 2.6 Magellan's circumnavigation of the world, 1519–22.

On Monday 8 September 1522, the *Victoria* finally limped back to Seville. Of the five ships and 270 men that had left almost exactly three years earlier, only one battered ship and 18 sick men returned. Magellan, himself, had died on the voyage, during a clash with a hostile tribe in the Philippines. The king rewarded Juan Elcano, who had captained the *Victoria* back home from the Philippines, with 500 gold crowns and authorised him to use the image of a globe for his coat of arms.

Thirty years after Columbus had set out to prove that there was a sea route to the spice islands of the East Indies, by sailing west, Magellan and Elcano had proved him right – the route did exist.

Interpretation 2

From *Rivers of Gold* by Hugh Thomas, published in 2003. Here, he explains the significance of Magellan's circumnavigation.

The world had been proved to be one planet. That the earth is a sphere was demonstrated. No greater achievement has been performed. It has been claimed rightly as a great Spanish triumph, and so it was.

Source E

Pigafetta was an Italian scholar and explorer. He travelled with Magellan and kept a journal of the circumnavigation. This is part of his description of Magellan's death in 1521.

A native hurled a bamboo spear into the captain's face, but the latter immediately killed him with his lance, which he left in the native's body. Then, trying to lay his hand on his sword, he could but draw it out halfway because he had been wounded in the arm with a bamboo spear. When the natives saw that, they all hurled themselves upon him. One of them wounded him on the left leg with a large cutlass. That caused the captain to fall face downward, when immediately they rushed upon him with iron and bamboo spears and with their cutlasses until they killed him. When they wounded him, he turned back many times to make sure we were all in the boats. Then, seeing he was dead, we, wounded, retreated as best we could to the boats, which were already pulling off.

Activities ?

1 Working in a small group, look carefully at Figure 2.6, which shows Magellan's circumnavigation of the world.

   a Identify the flashpoints where the expedition was in maximum danger.

   b For each flashpoint, decide (i) whether it could have been avoided and (ii) whether the right action was taken to move out of danger.

2 Compare your conclusions with those reached by other groups.

3 Now, working individually, write a paragraph saying whether or not you agree with the statement: 'Magellan's expedition took unnecessary risks'.

4 Who do you think should get the credit for the circumnavigation of the world: Magellan or Elcano? Discuss this in your group.

Summary

- After establishing the first Spanish settlement on the American mainland, Balboa discovered the Pacific Ocean, which he claimed for Spain in 1513.
- Pedrarias and Espinosa established the settlement of Panama on the Pacific coast, that linked with Nombre de Dios on the Caribbean coast.
- Velázquez conquered Cuba for Spain, at the cost of the lives of thousands of natives.
- A pattern was established that started with exploration – searching for gold and treasure – but then evolved into massacring and enslavement of natives – and finally conquest in the name of Spain.
- Magellan found a sea route to the spice islands in the East Indies by sailing west, and claimed the Philippines for Spain.

Checkpoint

Strengthen

S1 What were the key features of Velázquez's conquest of Cuba?

S2 Give two consequences of Magellan's expedition to circumnavigate the world.

Challenge

C1 An analytical narrative makes connections between events. Explain a connection between: the exploration of the Isthmus of Panama; the discovery of the Pacific ocean; and Magellan's expedition to find a westwards sea route to the spice islands of the East Indies.

C2 Now focus on Velázquez's conquest of Cuba, and make another connection between three events that took place during that conquest.

How confident do you feel about your answers to these questions? If you're not sure you answered them well, construct a flow diagram of the key stages in each event.

2.2 The conquest of Mexico

Cortes' expedition to Mexico, 1519

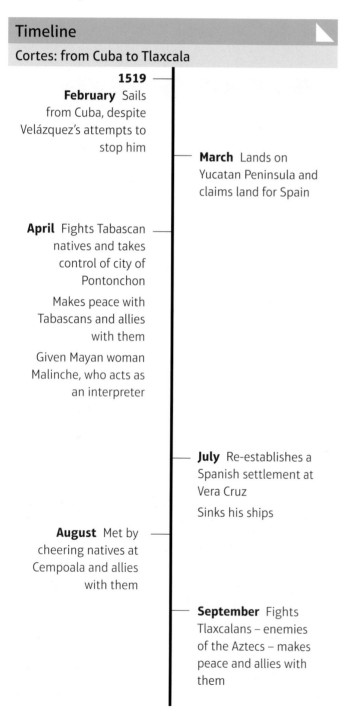

Timeline

Cortes: from Cuba to Tlaxcala

1519

February Sails from Cuba, despite Velázquez's attempts to stop him

March Lands on Yucatan Peninsula and claims land for Spain

April Fights Tabascan natives and takes control of city of Pontonchon

Makes peace with Tabascans and allies with them

Given Mayan woman Malinche, who acts as an interpreter

July Re-establishes a Spanish settlement at Vera Cruz

Sinks his ships

August Met by cheering natives at Cempoala and allies with them

September Fights Tlaxcalans – enemies of the Aztecs – makes peace and allies with them

In February 1519, Cortes (see page 44) set sail from Cuba with a force of 11 well-armed ships and around 600 Spaniards and other Europeans. They were soldiers and sailors, carpenters and sail-makers – as well as men looking for adventure and fortune. There were also over 100 Cuban natives, working as slaves to support the Europeans; about 20 women, to act as nurses, cooks and mistresses; and two priests. Significantly, Cortes took horses with him as well.

Setting up the expedition

Cortes' expedition was the third to the American mainland (after the expeditions by Pizarro and Balbao in 1509 – see page 39), but it was by far the biggest. This was for three main reasons.

1. Explorers, returning to Cuba in 1518, had reported finding cities on the mainland that were built from stone by natives called Mayans with whom they had been able to communicate. Significantly, the explorers also brought with them quantities of beautiful objects made from gold. This made exploring seem very appealing.

2. Velázquez, the governor of Cuba, was ambitious. He wanted to accumulate more wealth and extend his power and influence. He also wanted the glory and fame that would come with claiming more land for Spain, and praise from the Church for spreading Christianity.

3. Cortes had worked as Velázquez's secretary in Cuba, and as a magistrate in the capital, Santiago de Cuba, and had become a wealthy man. He wanted to extend his power and influence and, like Velázquez, please the Church.

Velázquez appointed Cortes as the commander of the expedition, with instructions simply to establish trading relations with the tribes living along the coast. Cortes was not authorised to conquer, or even to settle, on the mainland. However, just as preparations for departure were being finalised, Velázquez had second thoughts.

If he allowed Cortes to sail to the mainland alone, would Cortes ignore his orders and establish himself as an independent governor of a colony on the mainland?

Velázquez was aware that whoever conquered the mainland in the name of Spain would get fame, fortune and glory. He was aware, too, that his conquest of Cuba would look insignificant if Cortes conquered the mainland. Because of this, Velázquez intended to stop Cortes setting sail, have him arrested, and replace him with someone who he felt he could trust more. However, Velázquez was too late. Cortes, warned in advance, slipped away from Cuba with his flotilla* of ships.

Key term

Flotilla*

A small fleet of ships or boats.

Early contacts on the Mexican mainland

Cortes faced many problems when he landed in Mexico. Figure 2.7 describes these difficulties.

Source A

From Bernal Diaz del Castillo's *The True History of the Conquest of New Spain*, published in 1519. He travelled to Mexico with Cortes and wrote about his experiences. Here, he describes what happened when Cortes entered the city of Pontonchon.

We came upon a great courtyard, which had some chambers and great halls, and had three houses of idols. Cortes took possession of the land, for His Majesty and in his royal name, in the following manner: his sword drawn, he dealt three stabs to a large ceiba tree as a sign of possession. The tree was in the square of that great town and he said that if there were one person who contradicted him he would defend his possession with the sword.

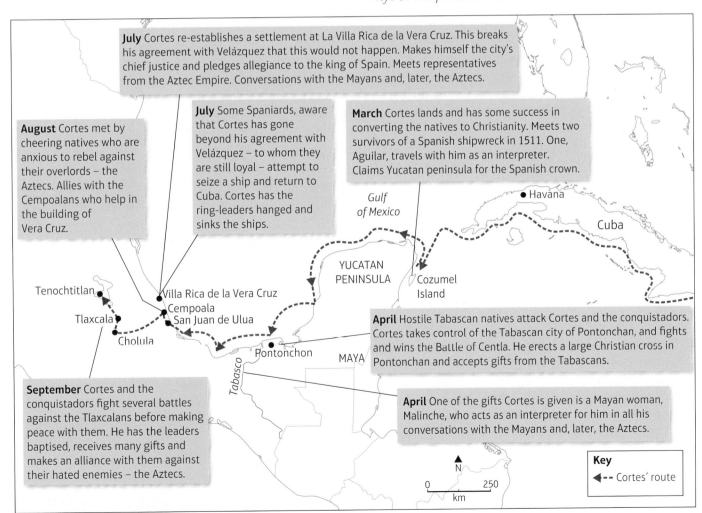

Figure 2.7 Cortes' expedition to Mexico, 1519.

Source B

A contemporary drawing, made in the mid-1500s from the *History of Tlaxcala* by Diego Muñoz Camargo, an official interpreter of the Spanish who had a Spanish father and Indian mother. It shows Malinche acting as an interpreter between Cortes and the Tlaxcala.

Xaltelolco.

September 1519: the situation

The situation, by the end of September 1519, was complicated for the Spanish for many reasons.

- Cortes was leading a small company that could probably be wiped out if the natives allied against them.

- Cortes and his men had no way of renewing their supplies or their ammunition.

- By sinking the Spanish ships, Cortes had cut off his line of escape back to Cuba, or even to Spain. The consequence of this was that Cortes had to remain in Mexico – he had given himself and his men no choice.

Sinking the ships was symbolic: it signified Cortes' commitment to exploring and conquering Mexico.

- The natives were afraid of Spanish firepower and Spanish horses, neither of which they had seen before. Many natives regarded the invading Spaniards as gods, and believed they were able to perform magic.

- It was generally the custom in Mexico to receive strangers hospitably. Cortes and his men had been given many gifts, as well as food. One of the gifts was his interpreter, Malinche, who was able to speak and translate Spanish, Mayan and Aztec.

- The native tribes fought each other as well as the Spanish. Many of the native tribes hated the Aztecs.

By the end of September 1519, it seems that Cortes had not decided whether to attack the Aztec Empire, or attempt to ally with it.

Extend your knowledge

Malinche

Malinche was the daughter of a native chief who had died when she was a child. Her mother married again and Malinche was given, along with 19 other girls, as slaves to the Spanish conquistadors. Cortes singled her out, partly for her beauty, but mainly for her ability to speak several native languages. This was invaluable because she could act as an interpreter between the Spanish and the different native tribes, especially the Aztecs. The Spaniards called her Dona Marina. She became Cortes' mistress and they had a son, Martin, in 1522. Cortes built a house for her and their son in Coyoacan, just south of Tenochtitlan. Malinche acted as interpreter for Cortes for several more years before she married a Spanish nobleman, Juan Jaramillo.

Activities ?

1   Read the section 'Setting up the expedition'. What do you think were Velázquez's and Cortes' motives in setting it up? Were they the same or different? Discuss this with a partner and decide whether you can prioritise them.

2   Now, working with the same partner, decide whether or not Velázquez was right to try to stop Cortes setting out.

3   Working in a small group of four or five students, put yourselves in the shoes of Cortes' advisers. It is the end of September 1519. Looking at your situation, what do you advise Cortes to do next – and why? Reach a conclusion with which you all agree. Now compare the advice you would give with that of other groups. How far do you all agree?

Exam-style question, Section A

Explain **two** consequences of Cortes' decision to sink his ships in July 1519.   **8 marks**

Exam tip

A consequence is something that happens as a result of an event. Make sure you focus on what happened as a result, not on the reasons why Cortes ordered the ships to be sunk.

The Spanish conquest of the Aztec Empire

When Cortes arrived in 1519, the Aztec Empire covered most of central Mexico. It was extremely rich and powerful, and was ruled by the emperor Montezuma from the capital city, Tenochtitlan. Yet in just less than two years, the empire had gone – destroyed by a small force of Spanish conquistadors.

The Aztec Empire

The Aztecs had been building an empire in Mexico for hundreds of years before the Spanish arrived. Steadily and mercilessly, the Aztecs defeated neighbouring tribes, extending their control. Rulers of conquered cities were allowed to remain in power as long as they agreed to pay tribute to the Aztecs and supply them with warriors when needed.

Some of the native tribes, for example the Tlaxcalans and the Cholula, were in a permanent state of war against the Aztecs. These were called the flower wars. They were partly ritual wars, fought according to a set of rules, and where warriors were able to display their skill in traditional, hand-to-hand fighting. A long-running flower war, however, could become increasingly deadly.

Extend your knowledge

Flower wars

These were wars fought according to a set of rules. They were called 'flower wars' because they were gentler than normal, aggressive wars. Aztecs believed that to die in a flower war was a more noble way to die than in an ordinary battle. A warrior killed in a flower war would go to heaven and live with Huitzilopochtli, the supreme god of sun, fire and war.

Source C

This plan of Tenochtitlan was printed in Germany in 1523. It was copied from a sketch made by Cortes. In 1519, Tenochtitlan was believed to have around 300,000 inhabitants and was bigger than any European city. It was built in the middle of Lake Texcoco and was reached by giant causeways [a road on top of an embankment that crosses an expanse of water].

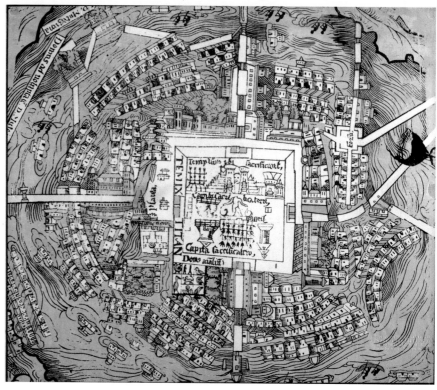

Aztec religion

Some Aztecs wanted to treat Cortes and the conquistadors as returning gods; others as dangerous invaders.

Aztecs worshipped many gods. They were usually connected to nature. The Aztec supreme god was Huitzilopochtli, the god of sun, fire and war.

Many Aztecs believed that Cortes and the conquistadors were returning gods.

Human sacrifices to the gods were common among the Aztecs.

Cortes and the conquistadors appeared from the same sea, and in the same spot, from which Aztecs believed Quetzalcoatl disappeared.

The god Quetzalcoatl was the god of life. Aztecs believed he had vanished into the sea and would one day return.

Figure 2.8 An Aztec drawing of the god Quetzalcoatl.

Montezuma and the Aztec surrender

Timeline

Cortes: from Cholula to the Aztec surrender

1519

October Cortes and his forces massacre 3,000 natives in the town of Cholula

8 November Cortes and his forces enter Tenochtitlan – welcomed by Montezuma

14 November Montezuma taken prisoner by Cortes – becomes a puppet emperor

1520

April Spanish troops arrive at Vera Cruz under instructions from Velázquez, intending to arrest Cortes

May Cortes leaves Tenochtitlan to oppose Velázquez's troops

Cortes' deputy, Alvarado, massacres thousands of Aztec nobles

24–29 June Spaniards trapped in Tenochtitlan as Aztecs rise against them

29 June Montezuma killed

30 June The Night of Tears: Spaniards are massacred as they flee from Tenochtitlan and spend nearly a year re-grouping and planning

1521

22 May Battle for Tenochtitlan begins

1 August Spaniards fight their way into the centre of Tenochtitlan

13 August Tenochtitlan falls to the Spaniards and the Aztecs surrender

Montezuma's Aztec spies had probably been tracking Cortes and the conquistadors ever since they landed on the mainland. They would have been reporting back to Montezuma on the progress made by the conquistadors. They would have been noting, too, the alliances and agreements made by Cortes with various different native tribes who hated and feared the Aztecs.

It was after Cortes and the Tlaxcalans became allies that Montezuma took action. The Tlaxcalans and the Aztecs had been enemies for years, and there had been many brief armed skirmishes between them. Montezuma was not surprised that his enemies were allied with the Spanish. He sent ambassadors to Cortes with gifts and an invitation for Cortes and the conquistadors to come to Tenochtitlan – the capital of the Aztec Empire – as his guests. The Aztecs urged the Spaniards to take a route to Tenochtitlan that would take them through the city of Cholula, which was under Aztec control. Was this a trap? Cortes decided to keep his options open.

He agreed with the Aztecs that he would travel to Tenochtitlan via Cholula – but he also accepted the Tlaxcalan offer to provide 1,000 warriors to go with him.

Massacre at Cholula: October 1519

Cholula was a holy city. It was not well guarded and had only a small army of warriors. This was because the city's rulers put their faith in their gods to protect them. This would turn out to be a mistake.

The massacre at Cholula showed the Cholulans that they could not trust the Spanish, and the Spanish that they could not trust the Cholulans. When it was all over, Cortes wrote to Charles I, telling him that 3,000 natives had been massacred and the city of Cholula destroyed. The massacre itself, and the fact that it had taken place in a holy city, sent shock-waves around the Aztec Empire. Cortes and the Spaniards were clearly a force to be reckoned with.

Cortes and Spaniards enter Cholula. They meet no resistance but are not welcomed with gifts and food.

The Tlaxcalans warn Cortes that he and the Spaniards have walked into a trap.

Malinche warns Cortes that the Cholulans are planning to murder the Spanish in their sleep.

Cortes meets the Cholulan leaders in the main temple. They admit that Montezuma had ordered them to resist the Spanish, but that they were not planning to follow his orders.

Cortes seizes the Cholulan leaders and orders Spanish and Tlaxcalan troops into the city.

The troops begin massacring Cholulans and set fire to the city.

Figure 2.9 The massacre at Cholula.

The taking of Tenochtitlan, November 1519 – August 1521

After the massacre at Cholula, a combined force of Spaniards, together with the Tlaxcalans and their own allies, advanced towards Tenochtitlan. They marched along the causeways (see Source C) and into the city as guests of the Aztec emperor, Montezuma.

- Montezuma, speaking through Malinche the interpreter, made a traditional speech of welcome to Cortes. Later, in a letter to Charles I, Cortes said he had interpreted this as a speech of surrender. Meanwhile, Montezuma treated the conquistadors like royalty. They were housed in his father's palace, given magnificent clothes to wear and feasted off gold plates.

- However, after eight days, the Spaniards, hugely outnumbered and isolated in an alien city, began to feel frightened and overwhelmed. They resorted to treachery and terror. They seized Montezuma and said

that anyone who opposed them would be publicly killed, cut to pieces and fed to the dogs.

- They forced Montezuma to act as a puppet ruler*. Montezuma was forced to rule the Aztec Empire according to Cortes' instructions. Cortes ordered that images of the Virgin Mary – the mother of Jesus Christ – who was worshipped by Christians, were put on top of Aztec temples to show that the Christian god was superior to the Aztec ones. During this time, Montezuma formally acknowledged Charles I as his ruler.

Key term

Puppet ruler*

A person who appears to be ruling, but in reality someone else is telling him or her what to do.

- In April 1520, about 1,000 Spaniards landed at Vera Cruz. They were not there to support Cortes. They were there to take him prisoner and assert the authority of Velázquez (see page 50). Cortes left his deputy, Pedro de Alvarado, in charge of Tenochtitlan and marched to meet the invading Spaniards. He fought them and won. Many of the surviving invading Spaniards changed sides and joined with Cortes. He now had a stronger force, more weapons, and more horses, as he marched back to the Aztec capital.

- Back in Tenochtitlan, with Cortes gone, Alvarado was afraid that the Aztecs would attack the Spaniards left behind. He therefore ordered the Spaniards to massacre Aztec nobles while they were enjoying a festival. Outraged, the Aztecs did what Alvarado most feared: they began killing Spaniards. Montezuma appealed for peace and was killed – probably stoned to death by a mob. Even the arrival of Cortes did not end the violence. On the night of 30 June 1520, the Spaniards tried to slip away from Tenochtitlan. They were caught. The Aztecs killed about half the Spaniards and thousands of Tlaxcalans and their native allies.

Extend your knowledge

The Night of Tears

The Spanish later called the night of 30 June 1520 'la Noche Triste', which means 'the Night of Tears'. It was called this because of the sorrow Cortes and his surviving followers felt at the loss of Spanish life and treasure. A story grew up that this was the only time that Cortes wept.

- Cortes and the survivors re-grouped with Tlaxcalan help between July 1520 and April 1521. They made alliances with the native tribes who lived around Lake Texcoco and were prepared to ally with the Spanish against the hated Aztecs. They then began the siege of Tenochtitlan.

- The Spaniards took control of Lake Texcoco early on, using boats they built along the shores. Then they took control of the causeways, fighting their way to Tenochtitlan. Once inside the city gates, they found thousands dead from starvation and disease after the siege. Those Aztecs that had the strength continued fighting. The Spaniards and their native allies made their way through the city streets, killing all the Aztecs as they went. Finally, on 13 August 1521, the city surrendered to Cortes.

In and around the Aztec Empire, people realised that the old days were over. Communities that been forced to submit to the Aztecs now resumed their old rivalries. Many of them turned to the Spanish to settle their disputes. Because of this, Spanish power in Mexico increased.

Figure 2.10 A picture painted in the 17th century by an unknown artist. It is called *'The conquest of Mexico by Cortes'* and shows the final attack on Tenochtitlan by Cortes and his forces.

Source D

From a letter written by Cortes in 1522 to Charles I of Spain. Here, he describes what he saw when his forces entered Tenochtitlan in August 1521.

The people of the city had to walk upon their dead while others swam or drowned in the waters of that wide lake where they had their canoes; indeed, so great was their suffering that it was beyond our understanding how they could have endured it. It seemed that more than fifty thousand had perished from the salt water they had drunk. The stench was vile. In the streets we came upon such piles of the dead that we were forced to walk upon them.

Interpretation 1

From *Conquistador* by Buddy Levy, published in 2009. Here he reflects on the clash between the Spanish and Aztec Empires.

The clash of these two empires [the Aztec and Spanish] is a tragic tale of conquest and defeat, of colonisation and resistance, and of the remarkable and violent confrontation between two empires previously unknown to each other. This clash of cultures in 1519 is the unbelievable story of one of the greatest conquerors that history has ever known, the complex leader of the civilisation he would destroy, and the cataclysmic battle that would be the end of one world and the making of a new one.

Exam-style question, Section A

Write a narrative account analysing the key events of October 1519 – August 1521 that led to the Spanish taking control of the city of Tenochtitlan.

You may use the following in your answer:

- massacre at Cholula (1519)
- the Night of Tears (1520).
- You **must** also use information of your own. **8 marks**

Exam tip

The question targets your ability to write an analytical narrative. Don't just describe what happened, explain the significance of the events.

Activities   ?

1 Read about the massacre at Cholula. Put yourself into the shoes of those who took part. Write two reports, of no more than 150 words each, on the massacre from the point of view of:

   a Cortes writing to Charles I of Spain

   b the Cholulan leader writing to Montezuma.

2 Look at Source C (see page 54). At first glance, Tenochtitlan looks difficult to attack and easy to defend. But is it? Half the class, working individually, must work out a plan of attack, and the other half a plan of defence. Now working in pairs – one with a plan of attack and one with a plan of defence – discuss which plan was more likely to be successful.

3 Working in a group, create a flow-chart of the actions that led to the taking of Tenochtitlan. Remember to include only the key events.

4 Working individually, write a paragraph to explain how Cortes managed to take Tenochtitlan.

Summary

- Cortes set sail from Cuba for Mexico in February 1519, despite the efforts of the governor, Velázquez, to stop him.

- Cortes landed on the mainland where he fought, and then made peace with, the Tabascan natives. They gave him a woman, Malinche, who acted as his interpreter.

- Cortes and the Spaniards, with the help of the Cempoalan natives, built a settlement at Vera Cruz. Cortes sank his ships.

- The Spanish defeated the Tlaxcalans in several battles, and then allied with them against the Aztecs.

- While on their way to the Aztec capital – Tenochtitlan – Cortes and the conquistadors massacred thousands of natives at Cholula.

- Montezuma, the Aztec emperor, welcomed Cortes and the Spaniards into Tenochtitlan, but ended up as their captive, ruling according to their orders.

- The Spanish lost control of Tenochtitlan and fled from the city. They then besieged it, and the city fell to them in August 1521.

Checkpoint

Strengthen

S1 Give two reasons why Velázquez tried to stop Cortes setting out from Cuba.

S2 What events show that Cortes developed good relationships with the native tribes that lived in and around the Aztec Empire? Find three events.

S3 Why were the Aztecs unable to defeat the Spanish? Find three reasons.

Challenge

C1 An event in an invasion can be significant because it changes the unfolding situation in a number of ways. Find and explain an event in Cortes' invasion of Mexico that either: significantly improved his chance of victory over the Aztecs; removed an obstacle to victory; or encouraged others to join his force of conquistadors.

C2 Choose an event after the massacre at Cholula that you think was significant in bringing about the fall of Tenochtitlan. Explain your reasoning.

How confident do you feel about your answers to these questions? If you're not sure you answered them well, put each event into a column headed 'Event' and 'Effect'. List one effect for each event.

Cortes as governor and captain-general of New Spain, 1523–28

News of the fall of Tenochtitlan and the collapse of the once-powerful Aztec Empire reached Spain within six months. However, it was not until Cortes' third letter to Charles I (see Source D on page 57) that Charles was able to give the matter his full attention. It was in 1523 that Cortes was formally given the title of governor and captain-general of New Spain*. This title was a formal acknowledgement of what he had been doing since the Spaniards had captured Tenochtitlan and enabled him, legally, to continue in his role.

But to Cortes' dismay, four royal officials were appointed to help him govern. One of them was given a secret code with which to communicate with the Council of the Indies*. Members of the Council had described Cortes as having 'crafty cleverness, burning greed and an almost obvious taste for tyranny'. For Cortes, this meant that he had to govern as Spain wanted: he couldn't do things his own way. It also meant that Charles didn't really trust him.

Key terms

New Spain*

This was the name given by Spain to the Aztec Empire conquered by Cortes, centred on Mexico.

Council of the Indies*

A council of Spanish officials originally set up by Ferdinand and Isabella to study the problems of colonisation in the Caribbean. It was based in Spain. By the time of Charles I, it exercised supreme power over the administration of Spanish lands in the New World.

Cortes' strengthens Spanish control

In the years to 1528, Cortes strengthened Spanish control in many ways.

- **He continued killing Aztecs, and the natives who had supported them.** In the weeks following the taking of Tenochtitlan, tribal leaders and high priests were hanged, and lesser officials thrown as food to Spanish fighting dogs. Other leaders were tortured to try to get them to tell the Spaniards where they had hidden gold and treasure.

- **Cortes took tribute from the remaining chiefs to make sure they stayed loyal to Spain.** For example, each chief in the province of Texcoco had to pay specific quantities of gold and maize. Cortes used Montezuma's records to decide how much had to be paid.

- **Tenochtitlan was rebuilt on the ruins of the old Aztec city.** Cortes ordered the destruction of the temples and other Aztec buildings that were left. He renamed Tenochtitlan 'Mexico City'. All the land he had conquered was named 'New Spain'.

- **Cortes allocated land to the Spaniards and set up the *encomienda* system** (see page 30). He encouraged Spaniards to bring their wives and children to settle with them. He kept many *encomienda*s for himself and his closest followers, believing that these were just rewards for conquering Mexico.

- **He encouraged exploration and the establishment of new communities.** Cortes believed this would strengthen Spanish control of the area, and allow the conquistadors to continue their search for gold. Conquistadors were sent, for example, to Zacatula on the Pacific coast, and to Oaxaca, the main gold-producing region of Mexico.

- **Agriculture was developed** by arranging for cattle, sheep, pigs and goats to be imported from Haiti. Cortes also asked for sugar cane, mulberries (for silk worms) vines and wheat to be sent from Spain. He aimed to free New Spain from dependence on other islands of the Caribbean.

- **Industry was developed** by setting up the manufacture of gunpowder. The discovery of iron near Taxco in the south west also led to the manufacture of artillery. The growing of sugar cane led to the production of raw sugar, and wool from sheep led to the beginnings of a textile industry.
- **Cortes helped the spread of Christianity** by asking Charles I to send out Franciscan and Dominican friars to teach the natives throughout New Spain about the Christian God and his son, Jesus Christ. Cortes asked for friars because he thought the calm and tranquil way in which they moved among the ordinary people would be likely to lead to successful conversions to Christianity. Hundreds of friars went out to New Spain in the years after 1523. They founded the Church in Mexico and carried out thousands of conversions.

Source A

Part of a 16th–century Spanish and Nahuatl manuscript. Nahuatl is the language that was spoken by the Aztecs. It shows the work being done by natives supervised by the Spaniards. The little speech scroll coming out of the Spaniards' mouths shows that they are speaking.

Extend your knowledge

Wheels

The only wheels that the Aztecs used were potters' wheels – they didn't use them anywhere else. They were amazed when they saw the Spaniards using wheels on carts, and in rope and pulley systems to lift heavy loads.

Exam-style question, Section A

Explain **two** consequences of the establishment of the Spanish *encomienda* system in New Spain after the fall of the Aztec Empire. **8 marks**

Exam tip

The question is asking you about consequence, so don't waste time explaining why the *encomienda* system was set up in New Spain. Think about consequences for the Aztecs as well as for the Spanish.

Cortes removed as governor of New Spain

Trouble was brewing for Cortes. He had made many enemies and they created trouble for him back in Spain. This led to him being removed as governor in 1528.

Factors contributing to Cortes' removal

1. **Velázquez became a determined enemy.** One enemy of Cortes was Velázquez, along with his supporters. First, Velázquez had tried to stop Cortes leaving Cuba, fearing he would try to set up a state in the New World that would rival Velázquez's in Cuba (see page 51). He had been right: Cortes had defied orders from Velázquez to explore and trade and not to settle. After this, Velázquez had tried again to stop him. He was behind the expedition that landed in Vera Cruz in April 1520 (see page 56). Cortes had to leave Tenochtitlan in order to defeat a force of Velázquez's supporters who had come to arrest and deport him.

2. **Rumours of greed reached the Spanish court.** Most conquistadors went to New Spain because they were in search of wealth. Rumours spread that the reason why the conquistadors had not found much gold in Tenochtitlan and other Aztec cities was because Cortes had stolen it all and kept it for himself.

Indeed, Cortes' secretary told people back in Spain that Cortes had a secret treasure chest filled with riches. Other people claimed to have seen Cortes open four large chests full of gold bars and jewels. Several people also claimed to have seen a special, private place that Cortes had for melting down golden objects. Royal officials began pressing Cortes to explain what had happened to all the Mexican gold.

3 **The king wanted to control Cortes.** Charles I and his advisers began to worry about the power Cortes was wielding in New Spain. As the king of Spain, Charles was the ruler of the New World, even though he had never been there. He needed a loyal and trusted governor of New Spain to carry out his orders and keep his interests in mind. For his part, Cortes was beginning to worry about the rumours his enemies were spreading in Spain.

For these reasons, in 1528, Cortes decided to return to Spain to explain himself. He took with him three sons of Montezuma and other sons of various native leaders. He took, too, a range of treasures: great Aztec feathered headdresses, cloaks and fans, jade jewellery, gold and silver. He intended to impress Charles I and his advisers. He did, but Charles was still worried, and decided that Cortes had to be controlled. He allowed Cortes to keep the land he had acquired in New Spain and confirmed him as captain-general, but not as governor. That post was given to one of Cortes' enemies. This meant that Cortes and the governor would never work together to exploit New Spain for themselves. Reports would go back to Spain if either of them thought the other was becoming too powerful.

The Aztecs under Spanish rule

In 1519, when Cortes first set foot in Mexico, about 25 million natives lived there. By 1555, there were only about 6.2 million left. Many had been killed in the various battles Cortes and the conquistadors had fought as they struggled to gain control of the land – but most of the 19 million who died did so after the Spanish victory.

All of the tribes in the area were affected, but studying the Aztecs provides an insight into what happened. Figures 2.11 and 2.12 show the consequences of Spanish conquest for the Aztec people.

Activities ?

1 Look at everything Cortes did after the fall on the Aztec Empire. Draw a Venn diagram consisting of two overlapping circles. In one, put everything Cortes did to benefit himself; in the other, everything he did to benefit Spain. Where do they overlap?

2 Put yourself in Cortes' shoes. Write a letter to Charles I, explaining what you have done in New Spain since the fall of the Aztec Empire. Use no more than 150 words. Remember that you are trying to persuade Charles that everything you did was to benefit Spain.

3 The Council of the Indies described Cortes as being full of 'crafty cleverness, burning greed and an almost obvious taste for tyranny'. Work with a partner to find examples of cleverness, greed and tyranny in this chapter. Then, individually write a paragraph to say whether or not you agree with the Council of the Indies' description. Compare your paragraphs. Have you reached the same conclusion?

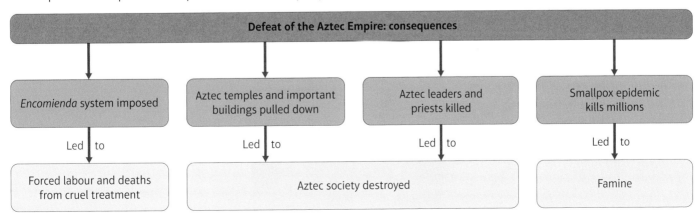

Figure 2.11 The defeat of the Aztec Empire: consequences.

The Spanish *encomienda* system was imposed. Thousands of Aztecs provided forced labour and many were worked to death.

The Aztecs had to pay regular tribute to the Spaniards in gold and other goods. They had to work even harder to produce what was demanded.

Many women became mistresses of the Spaniards and mixed race children were born. This caused complications when the legal wives and children arrived.

Many Aztec leaders were killed. The Aztecs had to find new leaders amongst the Spaniards who had taken over.

Tenochtitlan – the capital of their empire – was destroyed. A Spanish city was built on its ruins. In many places Aztec buildings were torn down and replaced by Spanish ones. This emphasised the ending of the Aztec way of life.

An epidemic of smallpox, brought by an infected sailor in April 1520, spread like wildfire. The Aztecs had no immunity against European diseases and millions died. Thousands of Aztec deaths meant that there were fewer and fewer of them to work the land. This led to famine.

The Spaniards forbade human sacrifice, tore down Aztec temples and threw out the priests. Aztec religion was destroyed and the people needed a new one.

Figure 2.12 Spanish conquest of Aztec land.

Source B

An Aztec picture of slaves laying the foundations of the cathedral in Mexico City in 1522. The cathedral was built on the ruins of the great temple in Tenochtitlan.

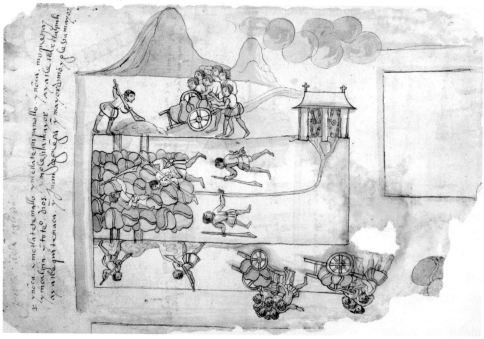

THINKING HISTORICALLY   Cause and consequence (2c)

Most events have multiple consequences. Their impact can often be felt in many different 'strands' of history: e.g. the Wall Street crash had economic consequences, but also affected society, politics and international relations. The fall of the Aztec Empire had consequences in several different areas.

1   How many consequences have been identified? Do you think this list is complete? If not, what has been missed?

2   Suggest a category (e.g. political, social, economic) for each consequence. How many categories have you ended up with?

3   Which of these consequences do you think Cortes might have had in mind when he was attacking the Aztec Empire?

4   Which of the consequences might a historian who is writing a history of the Spanish conquests impact on the Aztec religion **not** refer to? Explain your answer.

5   Write one historical question about the fall of the Aztec Empire that might require the historian to know about all these consequences in order to answer it well.

Effect and impact

The Spaniards destroyed the Aztec civilisation and society. In some ways what replaced it, despite it being Spanish, was very similar. However there were also new features.

- The Spanish *encomienda* system (see page 30) of working the land was very similar to the old Aztec way. Aztecs had to work for their tribal chiefs in order to produce goods that could be given as tribute to the gods.

- Aztecs were used to growing crops like maize, which they ground into flour, but they had never cultivated wheat, which the Spaniards introduced. The Aztecs also grew sweet potatoes, tomatoes, avocados and peanuts. However, animal farming was unknown to them: they had never used milk (they didn't like the taste) nor had they bred cows and pigs for meat.

- Franciscan and Dominican friars worked with the Aztecs to convert them to Christianity. Aztecs were used to being part of a society that worshipped gods, but were not comfortable, at first, with having just one god. Many kept their old gods while outwardly worshipping the Christian one; but many thought that the victory of Cortes meant that his god was superior to theirs.

- The Aztecs were used to being part of a society where there was a definite hierarchy, with the emperor at the top and ordinary people at the bottom. The Christian friars used this structure to spread Christianity. They worked first with the nobles, in the hope that, once they converted, the ordinary people would follow their lead.

- The Aztecs had books made from bark or animal skins. They wrote in a series of glyphs, which were little pictures. The Spaniards brought books with them and taught Aztecs the written alphabet that was used in Spain. This enabled Aztecs to document their own history in a language the Spanish could understand. It also meant that they were able to get involved in Spanish trade.

Activities ?

1 Study Sources A and B. They were both drawn by Aztecs after the Spanish conquest.

   a What can you learn from Source A?

   b What can you learn from Source B?

   c What are the similarities and what are the differences between the sources?

2 How might an Aztec have explained what he had lost as a result of the Spanish conquest? Write an account that will be kept by his family for his grandchildren to read and understand.

3 Draw two columns: head one 'Change' and the other, 'Continuity'. You can only put three things in each column, so choose the ones that were, in your view, the most important. Now compare your list with the students next to you. Use your list as part of a class discussion about what were the most important outcomes, for the Aztecs, of the Spanish conquest.

4 Genocide is the deliberate extermination of one race by another. Can what the Spanish were doing in Mexico be described as genocide? Discuss this in your class.

Summary

- Cortes was appointed captain-general and governor of New Spain in 1523.
- Cortes fell from royal favour in 1528, because he had acquired too much power, too much wealth and too many enemies.
- Spanish control in New Spain was strengthened by imposing Spanish systems on the native population.
- Millions of natives died after their empire had fallen to the Spanish and the fighting had ended.
- The Spaniards destroyed Aztec civilisation and society – although there was some continuity with the past in what replaced it.

Checkpoint

Strengthen

S1 Give three examples of the ways in which Spanish control was strengthened in New Spain.

S2 Find two aspects of Aztec society that were destroyed by the Spaniards, and explain why.

S3 Why did so many Aztecs die while Cortes was governor of New Spain?

Challenge

C1 Spain had considerable impact in the New World after the fall of the Aztec Empire. In your own words, summarise three key impacts.

C2 Explain the connections between the three key impacts you have chosen in answer to C1.

C3 Re-read the section 'Effect and impact' (page 63). Was there more change or continuity in New Spain (a) for the Spanish and (b) for the Aztecs?

How confident do you feel about your answers to these questions? If you're not sure you answered them well, write a thought bubble for how the Spanish behaved in New Spain, and one for how the Aztecs behaved.

Recap: The conquistadors 1513–c1528

Recall quiz

1 When did Balboa see the Pacific Ocean for the first time?
2 What was the name of the first European settlement on the American mainland?
3 Name the native chief who fled from Haiti to Cuba.
4 Who conquered Cuba for Spain?
5 When was the first circumnavigation of the world completed?
6 What did Elcano do?
7 Who was Montezuma?
8 Name the capital of the Aztec Empire.
9 When did the Aztec fall?
10 What is the other name for New Spain?

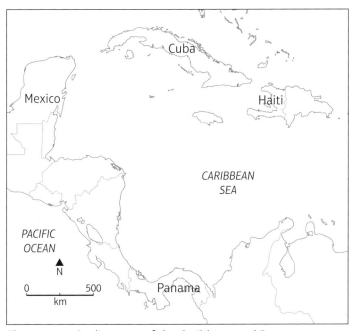

Figure 2.13 Outline map of the Caribbean and Panama.

Exam-style question, Section A

Explain **two** of the following:

- the importance of the circumnavigation of the world (1519–22) for the expansion of the Spanish Empire
- the importance of the Spanish conquest of Cuba for Spanish control in the Caribbean
- the importance of the capture of the Aztec city of Tenochtitlan for the settlement of Mexico. **16 marks**

Exam tip

Although three bullet points are listed, the question only asks you to pick two of them for your answer. You should pick the two you can answer best and write two separate answers for this question. Remember not simply to describe the event, but focus on its importance. Think about how the situation before each event was changed by the event, as far as the impact on the Spanish Empire was concerned.

Activities

1 Figure 2.13 shows a map of the Caribbean and the Isthmus of Panama.
   a Redraw the map, and using different colours for Balboa, Velázquez, Pedrarias and Cortes, colour the areas they added to the Spanish Empire.
2 All these conquistadors were linked in some way. Draw the appropriate arrows between them, and explain the linkages along the arrows.
3 Thinking about everything you have learned in this chapter, which one event would you argue was the most significant in the development of the Spanish Empire in the years 1513–c1528? Explain the choice you have made.

WRITING HISTORICALLY

Writing historically: linking information

When you explain events and their consequences, you need to show how your ideas link together.

Learning outcomes

By the end of this lesson, you will understand how to:

- link ideas clearly and concisely using present participles and non-finite clauses.

Definitions

Non-finite clause: a clause beginning with a non-finite verb. These can be any of the below.

A present participle: a verb form ending in -*ing*, e.g. 'running', 'building', 'forming', 'falling', etc.

A past participle: a verb form often ending in -*ed*, e.g. 'formed', 'happened', etc.; although there are several exceptions, e.g. 'ran', 'built', 'fell', etc.

An infinitive: the 'root' verb form, which often begins with 'to', e.g. 'to run', 'to build', 'to form'.

How can I link ideas using present participles?

You can structure sentences to link related ideas in a number of different ways. One way is to use a **present participle** to create a **non-finite clause**.

For example, look at all the different ways in which two sentences in the example answer below can be linked to this exam-style question:

> Explain **two** consequences of the establishment of the encomienda system in New Spain after the fall of the Aztec Empire. **(8 marks)**

| The encomienda system made grants of land to the Spanish. | + | The Spanish invaders made sure the land was worked for a profit. | = |

The encomienda system made grants of land to the Spanish, making sure the land was worked for a profit.

This present participle clearly and succinctly links the two points together.

1. Look at the sentences below. How could you link them using a present participle?

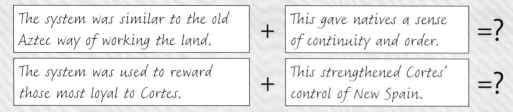

| The system was similar to the old Aztec way of working the land. | + | This gave natives a sense of continuity and order. | =? |
| The system was used to reward those most loyal to Cortes. | + | This strengthened Cortes' control of New Spain. | =? |

2. a. Choose **either** of the pairs of sentences above. How else could you link them? Experiment with two or three different ways.

   b. Which of your experiments expresses the information most clearly? Write a sentence explaining your choice.

How can I link ideas using other kinds of non-finite verbs?

There are three forms of non-finite verb:

- **Infinitives** (e.g. 'to open', 'to make', 'to mean')
- **Present participles** (e.g. 'opening', 'making', 'meaning')
- **Past participles** (e.g. 'opened', 'made', 'meant')

Compare the sentences below, written in response to the exam-style question on the previous page:

> *Cortes introduced the encomienda system. This meant he could force the natives to pay tribute to the Spanish encomenderos.*

This non-finite verb allows the writer to connect these two points much more neatly.

> *Cortes introduced the encomienda system, meaning the Spanish encomenderos could force the natives to pay tribute.*

Now compare these sentences below, written in response to the same exam-style question:

> *The encomienda system meant the natives could be worked hard. This meant the encomenderos made greater profit from the land.*

This non-finite verb allows the writer to connect these two points much more neatly.

> *The encomienda system meant the natives could be worked hard, making greater profit for the encomenderos from the land.*

3. Write as many sentences as you can linking these points using non-finite verbs.

> *Encomiendas could be passed from father to son.*
> *This encouraged Spanish families to remain in New Spain.*
> *This created a stable society.*

Did you notice?

Non-finite clauses can often be positioned at different points in a sentence without affecting its meaning.

4. Experiment with one or two of the sentences above, trying the non-finite clause in different positions.

Improving an answer

5. Look at the points noted below in response to this exam-style question:

> Explain the importance of the circumnavigation of the world (1519–22) for the expansion of the Spanish Empire. **(8 marks)**

> *Columbus had discovered the Caribbean Islands.*
> *It was not clear, from the Treaty of Tordesillas, whether they belonged to Spain or Portugal.*
> *If a Spanish explorer could find a way there by sailing west across the Atlantic Ocean, the Spice Islands would be Spain's.*
> *On 8 September 1522, the Victoria limped back to Spain.*
> *Their success meant that Spain could claim ownership of the islands.*

a. Experiment with different ways of linking some or all of the points using non-finite verbs.

b. Look carefully at all of the sentences you have written. Which ones work well, clearly and briefly linking ideas? Which do not? Use your findings to write a final redraft of the notes above, aiming to make your sentences as clear and concise as possible.

03 | The Spanish Empire, c1528–c1555

Francisco Pizarro's conquest of the Inca Empire, in 1533, happened through daring, cruelty and a good amount of luck. Pizarro's force of around 200 men should not have been able to defeat an Inca army of over 300,000 – but they did. Weakened by smallpox and civil war, the Inca emperor and his warriors were no match for the greed and treachery of the Spaniards. Despite an attempted revolt by the Inca people against Pizarro, the Spaniards were in full control of Peru and the whole Inca Empire by 1537.

The conquest of Peru enabled Spain to exploit the existing silver mines that were worked by the Incas. However, it was the discovery, in 1545, of huge new silver deposits that brought fabulous wealth to Spain. It also brought immense suffering to the Inca natives. Thousands died in the mines creating wealth for their conquerors.

The Spanish government needed to make sure their empire in the New World was governed in their best interests. The *encomienda* system was introduced and this gave large areas of land in the New World to the Spaniards. It also gave them rights over – and responsibilities towards – the natives who lived there. The Spanish government appointed viceroys in Mexico and Peru, along with a system of law courts and town councils. However, these did not always work well.

All trade between Spain and the New World had to go through the Spanish city of Seville. Consquently, by 1555, the city had become enormously rich and its merchants both wealthy and powerful.

Learning outcomes

By the end of this chapter, you will understand:

- the significance of Pizarro's conquest of the Incas
- the ways in which the Spanish Empire developed in the New World
- the impact of the New World on Spain.

3.1 Pizarro and the conquest of the Incas

Pizarro, Panama and contact with the Incas

Francisco Pizarro had been in the New World since 1509.

- He was part of an expedition that tried to establish a colony on mainland Central America. It was a total disaster. Pizarro was left, as leader, while they waited for Balboa to rescue them (see page 39).
- In 1513, Pizarro went with Balboa as he crossed the Isthmus of Panama to the Pacific Ocean.
- When Balboa was replaced as governor of Darien, it was Pizarro who was sent to arrest Balboa and bring him to trial (see page 42).

Pizarro was well rewarded for his loyalty to the new governor, Pedrarias: in 1519, he was made mayor and magistrate of the newly founded Panama City. With money, land, natives to work for him, and an influential position in society, Pizarro could have led a comfortable life for the rest of his days. Instead, he chose to continue his career as a conquistador.

Timeline
Pizarro's expeditions to Peru

Nov 1524
First expedition

Nov 1526–late 1527
Second expedition

1528 Governor of Panama refuses permission for third expedition

July 1529 Spanish Crown gives permission for third expedition

Dec 1530
Third expedition

First contact with the Incas

Pizarro's first expedition to Peru, November 1524

Pizarro's first contact with Peru was not a success. He and Almagro, his financial partner, with 80 men and several horses, only got a short way below the Isthmus of Panama – about as far as present-day Columbia. They did not find any treasure; Almagro lost an eye in skirmishes with natives; and the mangrove swamps* along the coastline put them off any idea of establishing a settlement. When they got back to Panama, they had great difficulty in persuading anyone to back further expeditions.

Key term

Mangrove swamp*

Mangroves are small trees that grow along many tropical coastlines. They form dense barriers for people trying to land. Their roots, partly in salt water and partly on land, make the ground treacherously water-logged.

Extend your knowledge

Financing expeditions

Those who led the earlier expeditions, like those of Columbus and Cortes, were paid salaries by the rich who funded their explorations and chose them as leaders. The ordinary sailors were paid, not in salaries, but with a previously agreed share of the riches found. Before long, international merchants and bankers moved in. They funded the start-up costs of expeditions and expected payment in an agreed percentage of the treasure found. As the enormous wealth to be found in the New World became clear, men began forming their own military companies, with each person responsible for finding and providing his own arms. Companies like this would choose their own leader – but might sometimes change their minds half way through the expedition.

Pizarro's second expedition to Peru, November 1526–late 1527

Pizarro's second expedition (see Figure 3.1) was an altogether bigger affair – consisting of two ships, 180 men and some horses. Almagro captained one ship, and Pizarro the other. After a couple of months, realising more men and supplies were needed, Almagro sailed back to Panama. Arriving there, he learned that the new governor, Pedro de los Ríos, would not authorise any further support for Pizarro – except to rescue him and his men.

Meanwhile, Pizarro agreed to let his pilot*, Ruiz, sail south, leaving Pizarro and his men on land. Ruiz and his men intercepted a large native raft that was going to trade with other natives. The raft carried hundreds of beautiful gold and silver objects, beads, jewels and finely embroidered cloaks and tunics. The Spaniards took three of the natives captive and seized all of the goods. Ruiz then sailed back to meet up with Pizarro, to show him that they were on the verge of discovering something big.

Key term

Pilot*

In naval terms, a pilot is a special sort of navigator, who can guide ships in and out of harbours and from ports to the open seas, avoiding all sorts of hazards, like sunken wrecks and sandbanks.

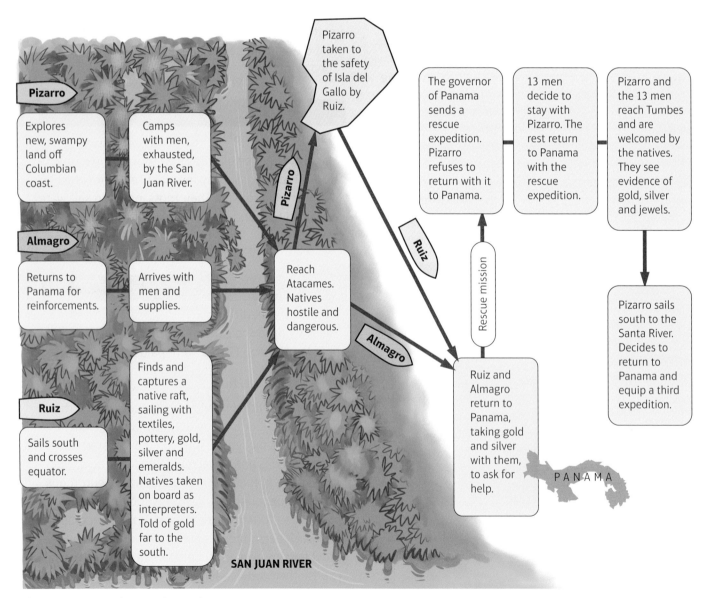

Figure 3.1 Pizarro's second expedition.

Meanwhile, Pizarro pushed on down to the San Juan river. He kept mainly to the coast, but he and his men made brief, quick expeditions deeper inland. What he found amazed and astounded him. He began to realise that he had stumbled on a civilisation that was quite unknown to the outside world. When Ruiz met up with Pizarro, it wasn't just the sight of the captured gold and silver, emeralds and pearls, that convinced him. He had caught glimpses, inland, of stone buildings decorated with intricate carvings. This civilisation, Pizarro began to realise, could be even greater than that of Mexico; once conquered, it could bring riches to Spain, and fame and fortune to himself.

However, by the middle of 1527, the expedition was in serious trouble. Pizarro refused to return to Panama with Ruiz, who was anxious to get more supplies. Instead, he asked to be left on the Isla del Gallo with his men. This was not a good decision. Marooned on the island with supplies of food running out, Pizarro's men grew mutinous. Meanwhile, Ruiz had been unable to get more supplies so that the expedition could continue. All the governor of Panama would authorise was a rescue expedition. When the rescue expedition arrived from Panama seven months later, only 13 men agreed to stay with Pizarro; the rest were only too relieved to be taken back to Panama. Pizarro pressed on, southwards, and reached the Tumbes region of north-west Peru. He, and his men, were warmly welcomed by the natives, and were amazed at the richness they saw all around them. The Spaniards received many reports of a powerful monarch who ruled over the land they were exploring – and of his fabulous wealth. They decided to return to Panama and set up a third expedition.

Getting permission for a third expedition

Getting permission for a third expedition to Peru was not going to be easy. The governor of Panama refused to give Pizarro permission. So, Pizarro set off for Spain to make a direct request to King Charles I. He took with him gold and silver, samples of richly woven fabric, as well as some natives and some llamas. These were intended to convince Charles that a third expedition would be worthwhile. On the evidence presented, the king and his advisers were convinced. On 26 July 1529, the king granted Pizarro a licence 'to discover and conquer Peru'. The licence gave Pizarro the governorship of Peru, with the rights to explore and conquer in the name of Spain and, significantly, a salary and the right to keep troops to protect the new colony.

Armed with all the necessary paperwork, Pizarro returned to Panama, where he assembled ships, provisions, conquistadors and sailors. He made certain that some of the Peruvians who had been captured on his second expedition came with him. They had become fluent Spanish speakers and would be useful as translators in meetings with natives. In December 1530, three caravels carrying 180 men, arms, provisions and 27 horses sailed from Panama – for excitement, danger and possible death, in Peru.

Source A

Pedro Cieza de Leon was a Spanish conquistador. He was a young soldier at the time of the Spanish conquest of Peru and later wrote about it, and about Peru, in four volumes called *Cronicas del Peru*. The first volume was published in 1553. Here, he describes what happened when the boat from Panama arrived on the Isla del Gallo to rescue Pizarro and his men.

Pizarro was downcast when he saw they all wanted to go. He quietly composed himself and said that of course they must return to Panama and the choice was theirs. He did not want them to leave because they would have their reward if and when they discovered a good land. As for himself, he felt that returning poor to Panama was a harder thing than staying to face death and hardship here. And he told them one thing more. He took satisfaction in one thing: if they had all gone through hardships and starvation, he had shared it with them. Therefore, he begged them to re-examine their options, and to follow him, taking a sea route to discover what lay beyond. After all, the Indians that the pilot Ruiz had seized said such marvellous things about the land ahead.

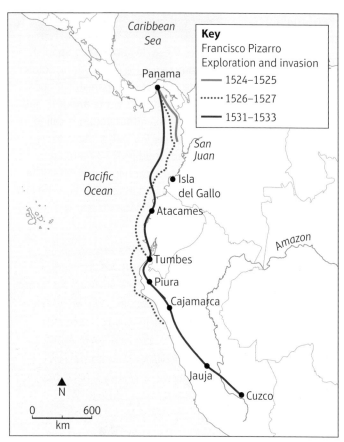

Figure 3.2 Map to show Pizarro's voyages of exploration and invasion.

Pizarro and the Inca Empire

At the time Pizarro was exploring Peru, the Inca Empire was at its height in terms of size and power. Its ruler, the Inca* Huayna Capac, had extended the boundaries of his empire either by conquering neighbouring tribes or by making alliances with them. By the 1520s, his empire covered a large part of western South America (see Figure 3.3). The Inca Empire was a rich mixture of peoples and languages, with different traditions and different ways of making a living. Not all of the different tribes were completely loyal; after all, some had been conquered and others had been forced into an uneasy alliance with the Incas. Some of the tribes, too, were occasionally at war with each other. Alliances between them were often formed – and just as often broken.

Key term

Inca*

One meaning of the word Inca is 'ruler' or 'emperor'. So Huayna Capac was his people's Inca. Inca can also refer to the people living in the Inca Empire.

The empire contained huge cities, temples and fortresses – with a network of well-maintained roads linking them; agricultural terraces – so that crops could be grown on mountainsides; and gold and silver mines. Huayna Capac, the Inca, was immensely powerful and was worshipped as a god by his people.

Interpretation 1

From *Conquistadors* by Michael Wood, published in 2000.

Behind Pizarro's twinkling eyes was a cool, calculating man who had already evaluated the societies of the Americas, and learned the... skills needed to survive as a conquistador. He was practised in deception and had the capacity to be unflinchingly cruel.

Activities ?

1   Read Source A and look back at the flow chart of Pizarro's second expedition (Figure 3.1). Draw two columns: one headed 'Arguments for returning to Panama' and the other 'Arguments for staying with Pizarro'. List as many arguments on each side as you can.

2   Compare your list with others in your class, and decide which arguments are the most convincing.

3   Pizarro failed to convince the governor of Panama that he should be allowed to lead a third expedition to explore Peru, but had no problem convincing Charles I that this would be a good idea. Write a paragraph to explain why this might have been. Think about Pizarro's adventures in the New World that the governor would have known about, and about Charles' 'bigger picture' involving building an empire.

4   While Pizarro was at the court of Charles I, he met up with Hernan Cortes (see page 44). Working with a partner, write, and if possible act out, the conversation they might have had. Remember that the year is 1528.

Figure 3.3 A map to show the extent of the Inca Empire in the 1520s.

The impact of smallpox

Smallpox (see page 30) had had a devastating effect on the lives of the natives of Haiti. This was because they had no natural resistance to European diseases. Smallpox did not stay confined to Haiti. Huayna Capac was just reaching the end of a successful series of wars in the north of his empire, and resting in Quito, when news came of an unknown disease that was sweeping

his capital city of Cuzco. Many of the Inca's family had died, as had his favourite generals and the governor of the city. Thousands of other people had perished, too. Alarmingly, traditional healers reported that their medicines were useless. This mysterious disease was smallpox.

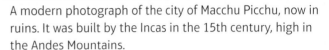

Source B

A modern photograph of the city of Macchu Picchu, now in ruins. It was built by the Incas in the 15th century, high in the Andes Mountains.

Source C

From Pachacuti Yamqui, *Antiquities of Peru*, published in the early 1600s. Yamqui was born and lived in a village south-east of Cuzco. He based his account on his own first-hand knowledge of the Incas and by talking with people who had lived through the Spanish conquest. Here, he tells a story the Incas told, that seems to foretell doom.

The Inca went to Quito to rest after battle, and to issue new laws and taxes. Then from Cuzco came news there was a pestilence of smallpox. And when he sat down to eat there came a messenger with a black cloak, and he gave the Inca a kiss with great [respect] and he gave him a small box with a key. The Inca opened the box and there came fluttering out things like butterflies or scraps of paper, and they scattered until they vanished. And this was the smallpox plague.

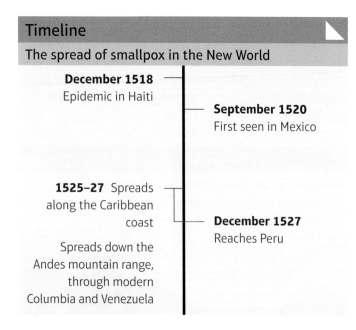

Timeline

The spread of smallpox in the New World

December 1518
Epidemic in Haiti

September 1520
First seen in Mexico

1525–27 Spreads along the Caribbean coast

December 1527
Reaches Peru

Spreads down the Andes mountain range, through modern Columbia and Venezuela

Part of the Inca's job was to protect his people from famine and disease. He needed to get back to Cuzco to consult with priests, wise men and leaders of the most powerful families. However, Huayna Capac had only travelled a short distance south when disaster struck. Smallpox swept through the army that was travelling with him. Generals and soldiers alike died; and then the Inca himself fell ill with a fever.

The significance of the death of Huayna Capac

The condition of the Inca worsened and his council asked him to name his successor. He left his empire to his favourite son, Atahuallpa, and to Huascar, Atahuallpa's half-brother. After Huayna Capac's death in 1525, Atahuallpa Inca and Huascar Inca ruled two separate realms within the Inca Empire. Atahuallpa held the northern part of the empire, centred on Quito; and Huascar, the southern part, centred on Cuzco. After a few months, civil war* broke out.

Key term

Civil war*

War between organised groups within the same country.

Atahuallpa should, by the end of 1532, have had complete control over the Inca Empire. His forces had defeated those of Huascar. Huascar was dead – murdered on the orders of Atahuallpa himself because

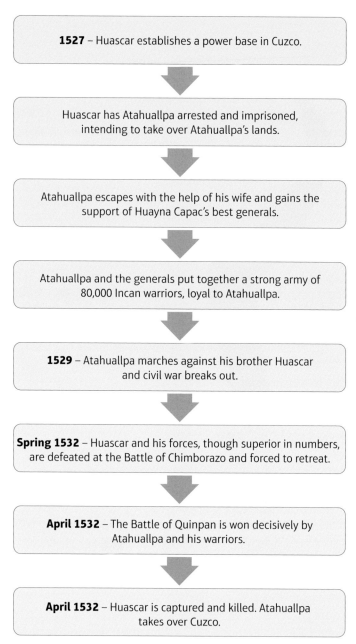

1527 – Huascar establishes a power base in Cuzco.

Huascar has Atahuallpa arrested and imprisoned, intending to take over Atahuallpa's lands.

Atahuallpa escapes with the help of his wife and gains the support of Huayna Capac's best generals.

Atahuallpa and the generals put together a strong army of 80,000 Incan warriors, loyal to Atahuallpa.

1529 – Atahuallpa marches against his brother Huascar and civil war breaks out.

Spring 1532 – Huascar and his forces, though superior in numbers, are defeated at the Battle of Chimborazo and forced to retreat.

April 1532 – The Battle of Quinpan is won decisively by Atahuallpa and his warriors.

April 1532 – Huascar is captured and killed. Atahuallpa takes over Cuzco.

Figure 3.4 Civil war in the Inca Empire.

he was afraid Huascar would ally with the invading Spaniards. The arrival of Pizarro and the conquistadors changed everything.

Pizarro enters Peru

Pizarro landed his third expedition high on the coast of Ecuador in January 1531, and spent seven months in the Puna region, getting his men used to living rough in a tropical climate. For the next few months (see Figure 3.2), Pizarro and his men moved down the coast.

They had frequent skirmishes with the natives, and word spread that these white men with beards were not to be trusted. They had not come in peace.

The expedition finally arrived at Tumbes. On Pizarro's second expedition this had been a thriving town; now it was ruined and deserted. He learned, through his native translators, that there was a simple explanation for this. The destruction had come about in the civil war that was being fought between Huayna Capac's two sons. Here, for Pizarro, was an opportunity not to be missed. Could he exploit the war between the two brothers? A divided society is much easier to conquer than one united against would-be conquerors.

Activities ?

1 Think about the sort of empire over which Huayna Capac ruled. What do you think were his greatest problems? Make a list, and then, with a partner, draw a spider diagram with Huayna Capac in the middle and the 'legs' being the problems involved in ruling such a vast empire. Are any of the 'legs' linked?

2 Write a paragraph to explain whether smallpox or the civil war was the greater threat to the Inca Empire.

3 Put yourself into the shoes of one of Pizarro's advisers. You have reached Tumbes and news has just arrived of the civil war amongst the Incas. Pizarro wants advice: should he stay put and strengthen his position by making alliances with native tribes hostile to the Incas? Or should he press on, down into the heartland of the Inca Empire? What would you advise him to do – and why?

Final steps to the Spanish conquest of Peru

In Tumbes, after listening to his advisers, Pizarro made up his mind. He gave the order to cross the Tumbes River and marched south, into the heart of the Inca Empire. The advisers had learned that Atahuallpa was heading to Cuzco; and Pizarro meant to catch up with him.

The Battle of Cajamarca

On 14 November 1532 – after marching along Inca-built roads, and making detours over mountainous tracks through the Andes – Pizarro and his small army of 180 men arrived above the Inca town of Cajamarca. Beyond the town they could see the vast camp of the Inca army: the smoke from thousands of fires rose in the sky. Importantly, Atahuallpa was still there. Pizarro had caught up with him.

At first, everything seemed to be going well with the conquistadors. Then it turned nasty – and followed the traditional conquistador pattern of talk, attack and destroy.

- Atahuallpa invited the Spaniards to meet him outside Cajamarca. He offered them the customary welcome of maize beer in gold cups. But the Spaniards poured the drink away, and they tried to intimidate Atahuallpa and the Incas by riding horses up close and threatening them. The Incas had never seen horses before. Atahuallpa himself was unmoved – and ordered all the Incas who had showed fear to be killed.
- Atahuallpa invited the Spaniards to meet him in Cajamarca's great square. There, they would be given lodgings in his palace.
- Pizarro and his men got to the square early. They hid themselves in the rows of pillars around the square and waited. At the end of the afternoon, thousands of Incas came into the square. Atahuallpa was carried in splendour to his throne in the middle of the square. Pizarro sent Friar Vicente to meet with the Inca and to give him a holy Christian book. Atahuallpa glanced at it and, asking whether this god was any better than the ones he worshipped, threw the book to the ground. Vicente shouted that the natives were against the Christian faith. This was the signal Pizarro had been waiting for.
- The Spaniards emerged from their hiding places and began firing into the crowds of unarmed people. More than 2,000 Incas were killed and thousands more injured. Atahuallpa was taken prisoner.
- The Spaniards pursued the Incas to Atahuallpa's camp and the killing continued. They ransacked the camp and came roaring back to Cajamarca with armfuls of gold, silver bowls and goblets, jewels and precious stones.

Source D

From the diary of Xerez, Pizarro's secretary, who was with Pizarro on his third expedition. Here, he writes about their arrival outside Cajamarca.

The camp fires of the enemy were a fearful sight. There seemed to us to be upwards of 30,000 men in the camp outside the town. Few of us slept that night, we just talked about what we should do. All were full of fear, for we were so few, and so deep into the land, with no hope of rescue.

Source E

Waman Poma was an Inca nobleman. He wrote about the Spanish treatment of the Inca people. His book *The First New Chronicle and Good Government* was written between 1600 and 1615, and was based on eyewitness accounts as well as his own experiences. The book was intended for the king of Spain. He never received it. Here, Waman Poma describes what happened at Cajamarca in 1532.

They killed the Indians like ants. At the sound of the explosions and the jingle of bells on the horses' harness, the shock of arms and the whole amazing novelty of their attackers' appearance, the Indians were terror stricken. The pressure of their numbers caused the walls of the square to crumble and fall. Desperate to escape from being trampled under the hooves of the horses, in their headlong flight so many were crushed to death. So many Indians were killed it was impossible to count them.

Figure 3.5 A picture showing Pizarro capturing Atahuallpa, painted by the British artist John Everett Millais in 1846.

The murder of Atahuallpa

Imprisoned by the Spanish invaders, Atahuallpa came up with a cunning plan. Aware that the Spaniards were desperate for gold, he made them an offer: his life for a roomful of gold and double that amount in silver. Pizarro agreed. Atahuallpa was moved to larger lodgings. Gradually, his original prison room was filled with gold ornaments and jewellery up to a line he had drawn on the walls. After eight months, the room was full and it was time for Pizarro to meet his side of the bargain and release Atahuallpa. Instead, Pizarro accused Atahuallpa of plotting against him and put him on trial for treason. It was a trumped up charge and everyone knew it. Unsurprisingly, Atahuallpa was found guilty by the Spaniards and sentenced to death. He was garrotted* in Cajamarca's central square, on 26 July 1533, as the Peruvians pleaded for his life. All the beautiful gold and silver objects were melted down.

Key term

Garrotte*

A method of killing by strangling the victim. Usually an iron or wire collar was put around the neck of the prisoner and gradually tightened.

Source F

Pedro Cieza de Leon was a Spanish conquistador. He was a young soldier at the time of the Spanish conquest of Peru and later wrote about it, and about Peru, in four volumes called *Cronicas del Peru*. The first volume was published in 1553. Here, he comments on the death of Atahuallpa.

It was the most despicable thing we Spanish ever did in the Indies.

Extend your knowledge

The death of Atahuallpa

Atahuallpa was originally sentenced to be burned at the stake. This horrified the Incas because they believed that to be burned to ash would deny that person a life after death. Atahuallpa agreed to a last minute baptism in exchange for death by garrotting.

Interpretation 2

From *Conquistadors* by Michael Wood published in 2000.

The Inca Atahuallpa was not an impressive character, and he did not handle events like a great king. But the manner of his death left an [everlasting] memory which, after his death, transformed him into a symbol of resistance in the Andean world [South America].

Exam-style question, Section A

Write a narrative account analysing the key events of 1527–33 that led to the fall of the Inca Empire.

You may use the following in your answer:

- the death of Huayna Capac (1527)
- the Battle of Cajamarca (1532).

You **must** also use information of your own.

8 marks

Exam tip

Plan your answer first by listing the main events that led to the fall of the Inca Empire. The question asks you to analyse the key events, so don't just describe them. Aim to make links between them. This will help you to structure your answer.

The Revolt of the Incas

Pizarro marched from Cajamarca to Cuzco, the Inca capital, and was welcomed by the inhabitants. Many nobles had hated Atahuallpa's rule, and others were glad the Spaniards had ended the civil war between Atahuallpa and his brother. They were reassured, too, when Pizarro had Manco – a younger son of Huayna Capac (see page 72) and half-brother to Atahuallpa – crowned as the new Inca. It looked as though Inca traditions were going to be respected and life would continue as normal. How wrong they were. Pizarro regarded the new Inca as a puppet ruler, who 'ruled' only under instructions from the Spanish. After three years, the Incas, under Manco, rose in revolt.

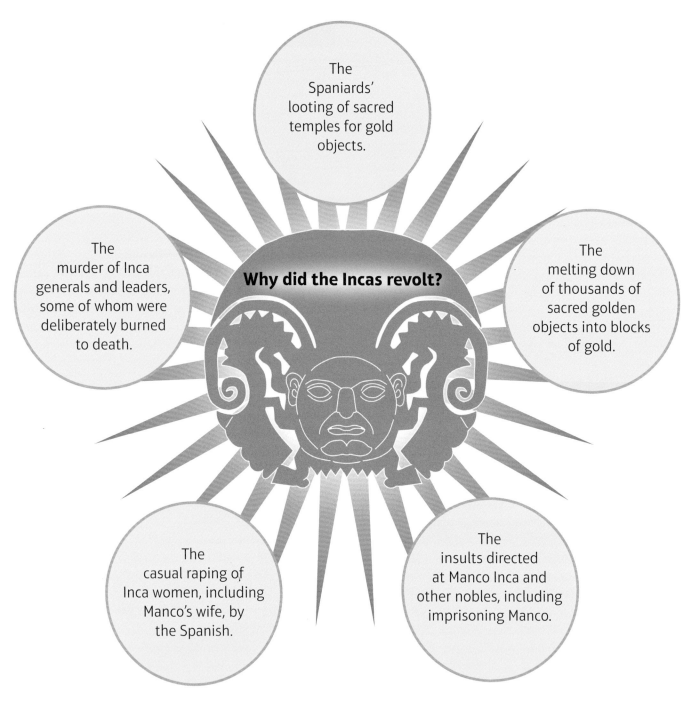

Figure 3.6 Why did the Incas revolt?

The course of the revolt

- Manco Inca escaped from Cuzco and gathered Inca forces at Calca, around 24km from Cuzco. The Incas made, prepared and collected weapons in secret. Manco had also ordered extensive crop planting so that his armies would be fed.

- In May 1536, tens of thousands of Inca warriors attacked Cuzco, which was defended by the surviving Spanish soldiers and around 1,000 natives. Manco ordered the city's water supplies to be cut off. His warriors stormed through the city, setting fire to everything that would burn, especially the thatched roofs. They then re-grouped in a massive Inca fortress overlooking Cuzco – called Sacsahuaman.

- The Spaniards, trapped in Cuzco, sheltered in one of the Inca palaces. It escaped being burned down because there were wells inside the palace compound. When the Inca warriors had gone, the

Spanish pulled down the burned out buildings, making wide passageways down which their cavalry could charge when the Inca army attacked again. Then they counter-attacked.

- The Spaniards terrorised the Inca civilians who were supplying the Inca warriors based in Sacsahuaman –they tortured and mutilated them. The Inca warriors, meanwhile, hurled spears, flaming arrows and rocks down on Cuzco. It became clear to Pizarro that taking the Inca fortress was the only way the Spaniards could win.

- The Spaniards mounted a surprise attack on Sacsahuaman at four separate points. They used scaling ladders to get into the fortress. The heavily armoured Spaniards, armed with European weapons and backed by their native allies, engaged in desperate hand-to-hand fighting with the Inca warriors. The fighting went on for several days, with attack and counter-attack. Eventually, the fortress fell.

- Meanwhile, Inca warriors were still besieging the city, trying to get the Spaniards out and kill them. This siege of Cuzco went on for several more months, until a Spanish force, under Pizarro's fellow commander, Almagro (see page 69), returned from exploring Chile and defeated the Inca forces in April 1537.

The Spanish were back in control.

The impact of the conquest

Pizarro and the conquistadors forced their way further into Peru, spreading death and destruction as they looted the riches of the country and established Spanish control.

Thousands of Incas killed or injured in warfare.

Millions of Inca men, women and children died from smallpox and other European diseases.

Incas forced to accept being governed from Spain.

Inca temples raided and stripped of gold; Inca religious leaders killed, and so Inca religious customs destroyed.

Inca golden objects, domestic – ceremonial and religious – melted down and shipped to Spain as blocks of gold, so destroying Inca culture.

Many Inca leaders killed, and other leaders submitted to the Spanish, so destroying Inca society.

Figure 3.7 The impact of the Spanish conquest on the Inca people.

Activities ?

1   It is 1532 and you are one of Atahuallpa's advisers. You are camped outside Cajamarca with thousands of Inca warriors. Spies have just brought messages to Atahuallpa to tell him that 180 Spaniards are marching towards Cajamarca. What do you advise him to do?

2   Draw a flow chart, starting with the battle of Cajamarca in 1532, that shows the events that led to Atahuallpa's murder.

3   Look back at Interpretation 1 (page 72), which describes Pizarro. Choose the events that support this interpretation. Would Pizarro have been so successful if he had been a kinder person? Explain your answer.

Summary

- Pizarro's first expedition to Peru in November 1524 was unsuccessful, but his second one, from November 1526–late 1527, found treasure.

- Charles I gave permission for Pizarro's third expedition, which left Panama in December 1530, and a month later landed in Ecuador and advanced into Peru.

- Peru was hit by smallpox in 1527, wiping out millions of men, women and children.

- Peru was hit by civil war after the death of the Inca, Huayna Capac.

- Spaniards took control of the city of Cajamarca in 1532 and murdered Atahuallpa, the winner of the civil war. Pizarro marched south and took control of the capital, Cuzco. Spanish control of Peru was complete.

- In 1533, Pizarro set up a puppet ruler in Peru, Manco Inca. In 1536, Manco led an unsuccessful revolt against the Spanish.

- Tons of gold and other treasures were shipped to Spain, with most of the gold melted down into blocks.

Checkpoint

Strengthen

S1   Explain why Charles I was willing to back Pizarro's third expedition to Peru.

S2   Explain two consequences of the Battle of Cajamarca in 1532.

S3   List the key features of the Inca revolt against the Spanish in 1536.

Challenge

C1   An analytical narrative makes connections between events. Explain the connections between the smallpox epidemic, the civil war and the death of Atahuallpa.

C2   A small force of Europeans, led by Pizarro, took less than six years to conquer the mighty Inca Empire. Not all of the factors that made this possible were equally important. Put the following factors in order of importance, and explain your choice:

a. Divisions amongst the Incas   **b.** European technology   **c.** Pizarro's leadership

C3   Explain what part luck played in Pizarro's conquest of Peru.

How confident do you feel about your answers to these questions? If you're not sure you have answered them well, draw up a timeline of the events of Pizarro's third expedition and annotate each event.

3.2 Expansion of the Spanish Empire

Learning outcomes

- Understand the significance of the discovery of silver in Bolivia and Mexico.
- Understand the ways in which Spain governed its empire in the New World.
- Understand the impact of the developing empire on the natives.

The rule of the conquistadors in the growing Spanish Empire was brief. They were adventurers who had taken tremendous risks to explore lands unknown to Europeans: some had made fortunes; others had died in poverty; and most of the leaders had met violent deaths. The government back in Spain did not fully trust them. In any case, the conquistadors had neither the ability, nor the desire, to run an empire thousands of miles across the Atlantic from Spain. The Spanish government had to put officials in place who could run the empire in the New World in the way the Spanish crown wanted it run. They had to be sure that the wealth of the New World was used for the benefit of Spain.

Extend your knowledge

The legend of El Dorado

Many conquistadors were inspired to explore in the New World by the legend of El Dorado. This was a story that circulated in the taverns and market places of Europe, and was probably inspired by the gold and silver sent back to Spain by Cortes and Pizarro. El Dorado was supposed to be a fabulously rich city hidden somewhere in South America – where even the streets were paved with gold! Local mines, it was rumoured, produced tons of gold and silver every year – enough to make men rich beyond their wildest dreams. In the years after about 1530, thousands of Europeans explored jungles and rivers, plains and mountains, in search of this mythical city that existed only in their imaginations.

The significance of the discovery of silver

The conquistadors were drawn to the New World by promises of adventure and the hope that they would discover gold and silver. The Spanish empire grew rich and powerful because men exploited the gold and silver that the conquistadors had found. This happened in three stages: see Figure 3.8.

Acquiring
Gold and silver objects were acquired either as gifts, through barter (exchanging for other goods) or by stealing. Most of the objects were melted down and formed into ingots (blocks) before being shipped to Spain. In a short time, all that could be found had been taken.

Prospecting
The Spanish began prospecting for gold. Many of them employed natives to wash out surface gold from streams and rivers. A lot of gold was found in this way, but it was wasteful of labour and an uncertain business; and it was only possible to find gold in this way – not silver.

Mining
In the 1530s, the Spaniards took seriously to mining. They took over existing gold mines from the natives. In the 1540s, extensive deposits of silver were found and silver mines opened.

Figure 3.8 The stages by which the Spanish acquired gold and silver.

Although it was the prospect of gold that drew the Spaniards to the New World, it was silver that was to bring the Spanish Empire the greatest riches. Silver mines were opened up and, in the 1540s, the silver sent to Spain formed 85 per cent of the total official shipment of gold and silver, measured by weight, and 40 per cent of the value. The quality of the silver improved, as new mines were discovered, and new techniques were used; and by the 1550s, the total economic value of silver shipments to Spain was greater than that of gold. The greatest and most important silver mine – Potosi – was found in 1545, in the Cerro Rico mountain of what is now Bolivia.

Miners and mining towns

Discovering rich veins of silver in the ground was one thing: getting the silver out was quite another.

- Effective pumps were not available, and so, initially, deep shafts could only be dug where there was little danger of flooding. Skilled workers were needed to decide where it was best to sink the shafts and open up the mines.

- A large labour force was needed – first to dig the mines, and then to mine the silver. Some of this labour had to be skilled, but most of the work was unskilled digging and carrying.

- The labour force needed food and water. Although food could be transported some distance, water, in sufficient quantities, could not. So the labour force had to be sited where there was fresh water available, and either supplies of food, or ways of bringing food in.

- Animals were needed to carry the silver away from the mines – either by pulling carts or, more often, in baskets of silver slung over their backs. Mules, donkeys and llamas were used, but they had to be found, brought to the mines, and trained to carry loads – and someone had to look after them too.

- Although thousands of natives were eventually employed in all the silver mines, there were some tribes who were hostile to the business undertakings of the Spanish, especially around the Guanajuato mines. So armed guards were needed to travel with the men and animal convoys who transported the silver away from the mines.

- Equipment was needed to smelt* the ore* to extract the raw silver before it could be transported; and, as with the mining, this job required both skilled and unskilled workers.

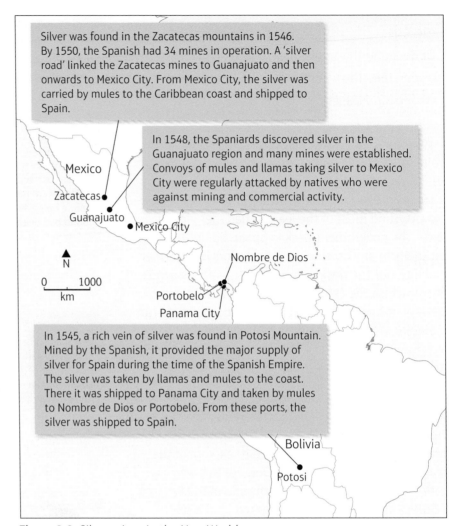

Silver was found in the Zacatecas mountains in 1546. By 1550, the Spanish had 34 mines in operation. A 'silver road' linked the Zacatecas mines to Guanajuato and then onwards to Mexico City. From Mexico City, the silver was carried by mules to the Caribbean coast and shipped to Spain.

In 1548, the Spaniards discovered silver in the Guanajuato region and many mines were established. Convoys of mules and llamas taking silver to Mexico City were regularly attacked by natives who were against mining and commercial activity.

In 1545, a rich vein of silver was found in Potosi Mountain. Mined by the Spanish, it provided the major supply of silver for Spain during the time of the Spanish Empire. The silver was taken by llamas and mules to the coast. There it was shipped to Panama City and taken by mules to Nombre de Dios or Portobelo. From these ports, the silver was shipped to Spain.

Figure 3.9 Silver mines in the New World.

Key terms

Smelt*

A process involving heating the rock until the mineral inside turns to liquid.

Ore*

The name given to rock that contains minerals – in this case silver. The silver is extracted from the rock by smelting.

In the late 1540s – as soon as word got out that silver had been found in vast quantities – a silver rush began. Europeans came from all over South and Central America to try to make their fortunes. Mining camps sprang up almost overnight around the Potosi,

Source A

An illustration of a silver mine in the Cerro Rico Mountain, near the city of Potosi, known at the time as 'the mountain that eats men'. This picture was drawn by Theodor de Bry and was printed in his books of illustrations called *America*. There were 14 volumes altogether and they were printed between 1590 and 1634. Although de Bry never left Europe, he based his illustrations on what he was told by the conquistadors and other Spaniards who had been there.

Zacatecas and Guanajuato mines. Here, too, were thousands of natives willing to work the mines and to learn the skills necessary. The mining camps were chaotic and disorganised, but were essential for the success of the silver mines.

Essential though the mining camps were, they never became administrative or social centres. They were too far from the sea and so too far from contact with Spain. The production of the Potosi mines, for example, was controlled from Lima, and the Zacatecas mines from Mexico City. The mine owners lived for much of the year in these major cities, running their mines through managers and foremen.

Much of the silver that was mined in Mexico and Peru went back to Spain, but much also remained in the New World and was minted as coins. As more and more Europeans came out to the New World, to work and to settle, money was needed to pay for European imports and to stimulate local trade and industry.

Interpretation 1 ⬤

From J H Parry *The Spanish Seaborne Empire* published in 1966.

It is not a great exaggeration to say that the discovery of Potosi was one of the turning points in the history of the Western World. Certainly silver became, in the middle years of the sixteenth century, the chief driving force in the Spanish economy in the New World.

Activities ?

1 a What do you think would have been the three most significant challenges for the owners of silver mines? Explain your choices.

   b Now compare your three choices with others in your class and arrive at the three you all consider to be the most important.

2 Imagine you are a Spanish banker who has invested in the Potosi silver mine. What arguments might you use to persuade others to invest as well?

3 Put yourself into the place of a native South American. What arguments might you use to persuade your brother **not** to go to work in the Spanish silver mines?

Running the Spanish Empire in the New World

The New World had been conquered for Spain by the conquistadors. These were soldiers and adventurers, explorers and fortune seekers. They did not necessarily have the skills that were needed to run a vast empire. Nevertheless, until the Spanish king and the Council of the Indies (see page 59) could set up structures that would enable their empire in the New World to be governed, the conquistadors needed to make sure they could hold on to what they had won. They were all far from Spain, and were a very small force of Europeans in a vast continent that contained thousands and thousands of potentially hostile natives.

There were three immediate and urgent problems to deal with. In the days after the conquest, they were problems that had to be dealt with by the conquistadors who were on the spot. In the months after the conquest, they were problems that the Spanish government had to deal with if the empire was to be run well.

1 **Make sure that there were enough supplies of food and water for the Spanish conquerors – not just immediately but for the future.** This meant that peace had to be restored and the natives given the confidence to return to their old ways of work. The natives were temporarily stunned by their conquest: their leaders and priests were dead, their gods destroyed, and their treasures looted. If central authority was not restored, they would just look after themselves and their villages, and not provide anything for anyone else. The whole system of tribute (see pages 29 and 30) had to be put back in place.

2 **Reward those who had supported and fought alongside the leading conquistadors.** Both Pizarro and Cortes had led brave and committed conquistadors. With victory, discipline relaxed, and the men began arguing amongst themselves. Some just wanted to return to Spain with a sackful of silver, and others wanted to continue adventuring. But most wanted a stake in the land they had conquered. They needed to be given this if the conquest was to become permanent.

3 **Set up an official and legal way of governing the New World.** This would legalise the initial arrangements that were made by the conquistadors. It would, importantly, make sure that the governing of the New World worked well, and worked under the Crown of Spain.

The *encomienda* system – together with the Spanish structure of government that was also set up in the New World – were ways of solving these problems.

The *encomienda* system

The *encomienda* system had been used earlier in the New World (see page 30) as a rough and ready way of rewarding conquistadors. After the conquest was complete, the system was imposed officially. An *encomienda* was basically a grant of land to a Spaniard, who was then called an *encomendero*. The area of land that made up the *encomienda* varied according to how big a reward the authorities thought the conquistador deserved, and on the type of land – whether it was fertile lowland, jungle or mountain. An *encomienda* could contain up to 2,000 native households. An *encomendero* could not act as he pleased toward the natives: he had certain duties as well as privileges.

- **He demanded tribute** from the heads of native villages. This was in the form of treasure or goods (and, later, money) and work. Work could be in the mines, in industrial projects such as smelting ore, or in agriculture.
- **He protected natives** from other natives or Europeans who might try to exploit them.
- **He appointed and paid** Christian priests who worked in the villages teaching the natives about Christianity.
- **He shared** the cost, with other *encomenderos*, of the military defence of the area in which they had their *encomiendas*.

The effects and importance of the encomienda system

- The Spanish *encomenderos* controlled all the land in the New World and had to manage their land following laws made in Spain.

- The land was worked to produce what Spain wanted: for example, cloth, silver and gold, maize and avocado pears.
- Natives were forced to work for the Spanish *encomenderos*, and, in this way, millions of natives became slaves.
- The *encomenderos* did not live on their *encomiendas*. They preferred to live in towns. This was because living on their *encomiendas* could be dangerous: they would be isolated and far from Spanish help if the natives turned hostile. This meant that the *encomiendas* were not always managed in the best way possible.
- The Spanish government allowed *encomiendas* to be passed from father to son. This meant that Spanish families stayed in the New World and, in doing so, created a stable society. It also meant that Spanish families could become 'little dictators' on their own estates.

The *encomenderos*

The natives

Figure 3.10 The *encomienda* system.

Extend your knowledge ◣

Cortes' *encomienda*

Most *encomiendas* contained about 2,000 native households. However, Cortes gave himself a huge *encomienda* in Mexico, officially containing 23,000 households – and probably many more. The *encomiendas* later granted by the Spanish Crown were much smaller.

Exam-style question, Section A ○

Explain **two** consequences of the *encomienda* system.

8 marks

Exam tip ○

The question is asking you about consequences, so you must think about outcomes. You must ask yourself 'What happened as a result?' Don't be tempted simply to describe the system.

Governing the New World

The leaders of conquering armies made certain that they either occupied the existing towns in the region, or that they founded new ones. They made these the centres of local government, with the conquistadors' loyal followers working as officers who made sure the different regions were run properly. This, though, was a temporary arrangement. It needed to be changed into an official and permanent government for the New World.

Council

- A **Council of the Indies** was formed in 1524. This was based in Spain. It consisted of a president and eight councillors and controlled all the administration, justice and religious matters that were to do with the New World. Members would discuss the dispatches received from the viceroys in the New World, summarise them and make recommendations to the king as to what course of action should be taken. Once a royal decision had been made, this would be sent back to the Council of the Indies, and onwards from the Council to the viceroys.

- The chief officers in the New World were the **viceroys**. There were two officials and these were appointed by the Spanish crown. One was appointed to New Spain (the name given to Cortes' conquests in Central America) and was based in Mexico City; and one was appointed to Peru and was based in Lima. The Peruvian viceroy was superior to the one in New Spain. Viceroys were the official representatives of the Spanish Crown in the New World, and were responsible for the ways in which it was governed.

- Government of the New World was managed through a series of town councils, called *cabildos*. The viceroy presided over the *cabildo* in his capital city, and appointed leaders to preside over the other *cabildos* in his region. The viceroys had tremendous influence and power. This was partly because of the distance between the New World and Spain. It could take up to eight months for a response to a dispatch to be received back in the New World, and so viceroys often had to take decisions before they were officially approved.

- The administration of justice was the responsibility of the *audiencia* **courts** and their judges. These courts administered royal justice in Spain and in the New World. It was the Crown's policy to separate the administration of government from the administration of justice in the New World, so that one could keep a check on the other. The courts were usually run by officials appointed by Spain.

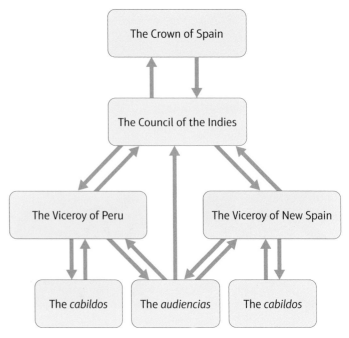

Figure 3.11 Governing the New World.

Activities ?

1 What were the immediate worries of the conquistadors, once they had conquered the Aztec and Inca Empires? Working with a partner, create a concept map linking the problems they faced with the solutions they arrived at. Remember that problems may be linked, and one problem may have more than one solution.

2 Explain the strengths and weaknesses of the encomienda system (a) for a Spanish encomendero and (b) for a native South American.

3 Write a paragraph of not more than 150 words to explain how the Crown of Spain controlled the Spanish Empire in the New World.

Improving the lives of the natives

Bartolome de las Casas

Bartolome de las Casas was a priest who travelled with the conquistadors to the New World. He took part in the conquest of Cuba, and was present at the murder of Hatuey in 1512 (see page 44), and at the massacre at Caonao in 1513 (see page 45). As a result of his loyalty to Velázquez, he was awarded an encomienda in the south of Cuba – rich in gold, and with thousands of natives to work in the gold mines and in the fields. Las Casas worked partly as a priest and partly as an encomendero. It was his work as a priest that led him to question the ways in which the Spanish were behaving in the New World – in particular their cruel treatment of the native population. He came to believe that, during the years of conquest, the violence that had been committed against the natives was morally wrong.

Concerned about the Spanish treatment of the native population after the conquest, Las Casas developed the view that, under the encomienda system, the natives were treated as slaves – and that this was not only morally wrong, but illegal. The native population should be protected by the Spanish Crown because they were Spanish subjects. If slave labour was needed, black slaves could be imported from Africa. Accordingly, in 1515, Las Casas gave up his encomienda and travelled

back to Spain. His plan was to persuade the king to abolish the encomienda system altogether, and free the natives to work where, and for whom, they wished. But matters did not go according to plan:

- King Ferdinand died in January 1516, before Las Casas could talk with him.

- The new king, Charles I, was too young to reign and regents took over the government of Spain until he was old enough to reign by himself. Las Casas told them about the cruel acts of violence that were being carried out in the New World – and he was appointed 'Protector of the Indians'. His brief was to advise the Spanish governors in the New World as to how the natives should be treated and to send reports back to Spain.

- The encomenderos would not change their ways, and the cruel treatment of the natives continued. Las Casas' cause was not helped by several native revolts, which convinced the Spanish that the natives had to be subdued and treated harshly in order to keep them obedient.

- Disappointed, Las Casas entered a monastery in Santo Domingo. In 1527, he began writing A Short Account of the Destruction of the Indies, in which he set down all the cruelties he had witnessed. He continued campaigning on behalf of the natives, travelling the New World, converting some to Christianity, and trying to persuade the encomenderos to treat their natives well. He had few successes.

Extend your knowledge

The peasant colonisation scheme

Las Casas developed a scheme for setting up townships in which the natives would govern themselves; and, alongside this, a scheme encouraging peasants to leave Spain and work with the natives – showing them how to work the land as free people. Both these schemes failed. Spanish colonists opposed the township idea, and the natives were hostile to the Spanish peasants.

The New Laws, 1542

By 1540, the situation had changed. King Charles I was now an extremely powerful ruler, not just of Spain, but of the Netherlands as well. The Spanish treasury was dependent on silver and gold from the New World, and it was essential that these supplies were maintained. Thousands of natives had already died, but an effective native labour force was vital to Spanish wealth.

In 1542, Bartolome de las Casas returned to Spain to argue on behalf of the natives once more. Before a committee, consisting mainly of members of the Council of the Indies, he argued that the only way forward was to end the *encomienda* system and put all natives under the protection of the Crown. They would become tribute-paying subjects of Spain. This time, Las Casas' arguments – supported by his eyewitness accounts of Spanish violence – were successful. On 20 November 1542, Charles I signed the New Laws, which:

- made it illegal to force natives to work if they didn't want to
- banned the capture of natives just so that they could become slaves
- allowed reasonable tribute to be collected by the *encomenderos*, but stated that all other work had to be paid for
- started the gradual ending of the *encomienda* system by stating that every *encomienda* had to be given to the Crown on the death of the current *encomendero*.

The New Laws did not go down well in the New World. The viceroy of New Spain, himself an *encomendero*, refused to implement them; and in Peru, a serious rebellion broke out in 1544, led by Gonzalo Pizarro, the brother of Francisco Pizarro. The Peruvian viceroy was killed, and Gonzalo Pizarro was so successful that he ruled Peru for two years before another Spanish army captured and executed him. A second rebellion broke out, but was put down.

Charles I came so close to losing Peru during the conquistador uprisings that his councillors advised him to suspend most of the New Laws. This he did, but insisted on keeping the requirement that *encomiendas* reverted to the Crown on the death of the *encomendero*.

Once this happened, the *encomiendas* were run by agents appointed by the Spanish Crown, but working for themselves. They were appointed for short periods, and so tended to squeeze as much profit as they could from the land. The working lives of many of the natives did not improve (see Source B below).

> ## Source B
>
> From *A Short History of the Destruction of the Indies* written by Bartolome de las Casas, in 1542. Here he is describing the reaction in the New World to the New Laws.
>
> *In many parts of the New World men have taken the law into their own hands and, while pretending to observe the New Laws, are now in fact in open revolt. They have all been extremely reluctant to give up the position and wealth they have won for themselves during their life of crime, and unwilling to free the natives they have acquired and condemned to [everlasting] slavery. Now they no longer murder the natives on sight, they have got into the habit of killing them slowly with hard labour.*

> ## Activities ?
>
> 1 Working with a partner, one of you take on the role of an *encomendero*, and the other, the role of Bartolome de las Casas. Create a discussion between the two men in which they try to persuade each other of their views about the treatment of the natives.
> 2 Explain why the New Laws didn't work as Charles I intended them to.

The founding of La Paz, 1548

In 1548, the Spanish built the city of La Paz (in modern Bolivia) to commemorate the restoration of peace after the rebellion led by Gonzalo Pizarro. It was built on the site of the Inca city of Laja that the Spaniards had destroyed. The position of La Paz was significant: it was built at the connecting point between the routes that led from the silver mines of Potosi and Oruro, to Lima. The city gradually became the administrative centre of the Spanish empire in South America.

Source C

A modern photograph of Iglesia de San Francisco, La Paz, built in the 16th century.

Summary

- Silver mines were opened up in Peru in the 1540s.
- The problems involved in getting silver out of the ground led to the establishment of mining towns.
- Silver became more important and worth more than gold as an export from Peru – especially after the opening of the Potosi silver mine in 1545.
- The *encomienda* system granted land to Spaniards in the New World. This carried rights and responsibilities towards the natives.
- The Spanish government appointed viceroys in Peru and Mexico, who governed in their name and were answerable to the Council of the Indies, based in Spain.
- Bartolome de las Casas, a Dominican priest, alerted the Spanish government to the acts of violence that were being committed by the Spanish against the natives in the New World.
- The Spanish government passed the New Laws, aiming to stop the natives being used as slaves and to bring a gradual end to the *encomienda* system.
- Opposition to the New Laws led to revolts in the New World, which resulted in the New Laws being relaxed.

Checkpoint

Strengthen

S1 Describe how the problems in mining silver were overcome.

S2 Describe the main features of the *encomienda* system.

S3 Explain why the New Laws were so unpopular in the New World

Challenge

C1 Explain the importance of Bartolome de las Casas.

C2 Explain the problems faced by the Spanish government as they tried to govern their empire in the New World.

How confident do you feel about your answers to these questions? To build your confidence about the period, practise making links between events. For example, what was the connection between Bartolome de las Casas and the New Laws?

The impact Spain had on the New World was clear. The Aztec and Inca civilisations were wiped out. Native cultures and civilisations were destroyed. Millions of natives died as a result of the Spanish invasions. But what impact did the New World have on Spain? The most significant change was brought about by the huge amount of bullion* – gold and silver – that entered Spain from the 1520s onwards.

Key term

Bullion*

A word that refers to all kinds treasure – but mainly gold and silver.

The impact of gold and silver on the Spanish economy

The Spanish exploration of the New World was largely driven by the desire to find gold and silver. This was important because the gold and silver – particularly the silver – was used to make coins. Because of their high silver content, Spanish coins were widely accepted in Europe. Spanish merchants were able to trade easily with the rest of Europe, and many became extremely rich – as did the Crown.

Extend your knowledge

'Pieces of eight'

In books, films and pantomimes, you might have come across 'pirates' searching for silver coins that they call 'pieces of eight'. This phrase has its roots in history: a Spanish *peso* was made up of eight coins of lesser value. So a *peso* was, literally, pieces of eight.

This was not necessarily a good thing, in the long term, for the Spanish economy:

- Because the Spanish had so much gold and silver coin, they bought the goods they needed from other European countries, rather than investing it in developing industries in Spain. Indeed, there was little incentive to do this: why invest money long-term in developing machinery to produce goods when you had plenty of money to buy them, ready-made? This meant that the English cloth industry, for example, grew and flourished in order to meet the demand from Spain.

- Aware that wealth was pouring into Spain, and that Spanish merchants could afford to pay high prices for what they wanted, European traders put up their prices. They also put up their prices because the Spanish demand for goods created temporary shortages. This meant that, when these goods were sold on in Spain, the Spanish merchants passed on the price rise – causing inflation*. Poorer people started to find they couldn't afford imported goods, so they started demanding higher wages to compensate.

- The Spanish crown took about 25 per cent of the bullion coming into Spain. Instead of investing it in Spanish industry and business, Charles I invested it in the military. Spain had a large European empire that included parts of the Netherlands and Italy. This needed defending against Spain's enemies – particularly France.

- Some of the wealth coming into the Spanish Crown was spent in the New World. This was mainly spent on protecting the existing gold and silver mines – making sure that non-Spanish Europeans didn't have access to them. Money had to be spent, too, on providing armed ships to protect the Spanish treasure fleets sailing across the Atlantic back to Spain.

Key term

Inflation*

A situation where prices rise more quickly than wages.

The basic problem for the Spanish economy was that, instead of getting wealthy by making something and selling it, Spaniards were getting wealthy by finding bullion.

Figure 3.12 How should bullion from the New World be spent?

Attacks on the treasure routes to Spain

Right from the start, ships moving to and from the New World rarely sailed alone. By sailing in small groups, they provided each other with security if they were attacked or if the weather turned foul. They also shared navigational knowledge. Experienced navigators were few – and even the best sometimes made mistakes. Everyone felt safer when navigational officers consulted with each other. Even so, these precautions were of no help when it came to attacks by pirates or privateers*, desperate for the silver carried by the treasure ships.

> **Key term**
>
> **Privateers***
>
> Private ships that were licensed by rival governments to attack, sink or capture enemy ships.

Pirates and privateers

Sailing ships used routes through the Caribbean and across the Atlantic that were largely determined by the trade winds. These could be relied upon to blow steadily (see Figure 3.13). Sailing usually took place in the summer months in order to avoid winter storms; and, because of the trade winds, the ships took well-defined and predictable routes. This left them in constant danger of attack. Attacks came from enemy fighting ships during wartime; by privateers funded by hostile governments during times of tension; and by pirates at any time. If successful, the privateer kept a previously agreed portion of the treasure and their government got the rest. Pirates, of course, took everything they could for themselves.

Spain's control of New World bullion created tension with other European countries – in particular with France. French privateers began attacking Spanish treasure ships as they neared the coast of Spain. In this way, the French government claimed some of the New World treasure without having to openly attack Spain. In 1522, in an attempt to stop this, the Spanish government sent a fleet of warships into the Atlantic Ocean to escort the returning ships into port. France responded by licensing privateers to operate far out in the Atlantic Ocean. This had some success: in 1537, for example, French privateers captured nine Spanish treasure ships. Full-scale war with France broke out in 1542, and attacks on the Spanish treasure fleets intensified. Spain felt that something had to be done.

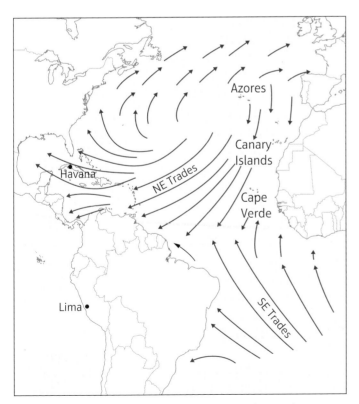

Figure 3.13 Summer trade winds in the northern Atlantic Ocean.

Convoys and fleets

During the war with France (1542–46), Spain adapted ships and developed systems to protect their fleets.

- Galleons were developed and built. These were large fighting ships about 32 metres long and 10 metres wide, with three or four masts, two or three decks, and between 24 and 36 cannon that could fire broadside*.

- The galleons patrolled the sea routes, keeping them free of enemy ships. They also sailed with groups of unarmed ships in order to protect them from attack.

- Because they were heavily armed, galleons started carrying the treasure that was due to the Crown.

- Spain developed a treasure fleet system. It created two main fleets: the *Tierra Firme* and the *New Spain*. They sailed, usually together, to the New World, protected by armed galleons, and following the same route to the Caribbean. Once there, the *Tierra Firme* fleet turned south for South America and the *New Spain* fleet went on to Mexico. The fleets usually wintered in the Caribbean before meeting up in Havana and sailing back to Spain. They left Havana in the spring, trying to avoid winter storms and late summer hurricanes.

- The government put a tax on the goods that were carried in the treasure fleets. The tax varied according to the value of the goods. Silver and gold, for example, were taxed at 20 per cent of their value. The money was used to pay for the warships that protected the convoys. In order to avoid paying the tax, smuggling was common. Warships often carried illegal cargoes that belonged to the admirals, captains and their staff. Some of them made a fortune in this way.

Key term

Broadside*

A ship firing broadside fired its canons from the sides of the ship. The canons were usually placed on a gun deck – which was one or two decks below the surface deck – and fired through portholes (openings along the sides of the ship).

Activities ?

1   Look at Figure 3.12 and select one of the individuals. Taking the point he is making as your starting point, develop an argument for his point of view in not more than 100 words.

2   Draw two columns: one headed 'Dangers faced by the treasure fleets', and one headed 'Actions taken to make the voyages safer'. List as many features as you can in each column. Draw lines to connect the factors in each column. Remember that actions may link to more than one danger.

3   Design a poster encouraging people to work on the treasure fleets.

Source A

A contemporary engraving, dated about 1550, of a Spanish galleon.

The impact on Spain of trade with the New World

The focus of all Spanish trade to and from the New World was the city of Seville. The impact on Spain of trade with the New World was felt first in Seville and then spread throughout Spain.

Seville: the hub of trade with the New World

Seville was an inland port in the south of Spain, situated about 100km up a small river. This was both a strength and a weakness. It was a weakness because the river was slow and sluggish and sometime got blocked with mud; large ships struggled to reach Seville and sometimes wrecks made the journey even more difficult. Seville's situation was also a strength, because it was more or less safe from enemy attack by water.

Seville had become the most prosperous city in the western world. Merchants grew prosperous trading through Seville. They also grew wealthy in other ways.

The slave trade

The deaths of thousands and thousands of natives in the New World created a demand for labour. Bartolome de las Casas (see page 87) had suggested that native labour was replaced by black slave labour – though he later said any slave labour was wrong. However, the problem of acquiring slave labour went back to 1494 and the Treaty of Tordesillas (see page 25). This meant that the Spanish in the New World could not go to Africa for slaves and buy them from the Portuguese. Similarly, the Portuguese in Africa could not sell slaves directly to the Spanish in the New World. In order to get around this problem, in 1518, the Spanish government began issuing *asientos*. An *asiento* was a licence to supply a specified number of black African slaves to colonists in the New World. The *asientos* were sold to the merchants who could offer the most money for them. The Spanish merchants who bought the licences could buy black Africans from Africa and sell them in the Spanish Empire – at a profit. Merchants could also sell the licences, or shares in the licences, to other merchants. In this way – as well as by importing bullion and goods from the Spanish Empire – Spanish merchants grew extremely wealthy.

Power and control: the Casa de Contratacion

In 1503, Queen Isabella ordered the setting up of the *Casa de Contratacion* (House of Trade, see page 31). By 1555, Seville still had the monopoly on trade with the New World. All the goods imported from the New World had to pass through Seville's *Casa de Contratacion*. Since Seville was the only Spanish port from which ships could sail to the New World, merchants from all over Europe had to travel there in order to buy goods from the New World, or to bring goods that they wanted to sell in the New World.

In 1543, a merchants' guild, the *Consulado de Mercaderes**, was founded, after pressure from the merchants to be involved in the work of the *Casa de*

Contratacion. Together, these two organisations controlled most of the trade in the Spanish colonies. So they were able to keep hold of their monopoly there and keep prices high. The control of trade and prices meant that, together, they grew very rich and powerful.

Key term

Consulado de Mercaderes*

A merchants' guild that worked with the *Casa de Contratacion* to control trade with the New World. A guild was a union of workers in a particular trade or occupation – in this case, merchants.

The treasure ships unloaded gold, silver and pearls that were taken by carts to the royal warehouses.

Oil, wine, glass and fine silks were loaded onto ships that were getting ready to sail west to the New World.

Cows, pigs, horses and chickens, were among the animals shipped from Spain to the New World.

The open-air markets were busy selling tomatoes and tobacco, peppers and avocado pears, kidney beans and potatoes – all of which had been imported from the New World.

Merchants had warehouses full of woollen cloth, skins and furs, fine china and delicate lace.

Some merchants were extremely rich and had built fine houses for themselves and their families.

Figure 3.14 The wealth of Seville. The picture of the docks was painted in the 1500s by an unknown artist and shows the wealth of goods coming into the city. By 1555, Seville was a rich and exciting port.

Governing the New World

By 1555, the Spanish government in Cadiz had developed a system of government and control in the New World.

- The Council of the Indies (see page 59), set up and working in Cadiz, was responsible for making sure the New World was governed well. Members received reports from the viceroys and used these to inform the king about the situation in the New World. The Council advised the king on what action should be taken, and informed the viceroys what should be done.

- The two viceroys, based in Mexico and Peru (see page 86), were responsible to the Council of the Indies for the good government of the New World – and through the Council they were responsible to the Crown.

- The Spanish system of *audiencia* courts was set up in the New World, with judges and court officials appointed by the Crown. This made sure that Spanish justice was administered in the New World.

- The Spanish *encomienda* system made sure that Spaniards owned all the land in the New World, and that it was worked for the benefit of Spain.

- The *Casa de Contratacion* controlled all trade with Spain. It made sure that trade was carried in Spanish ships, and that Seville became the only Spanish port through which trade could pass.

- The Spanish government developed and protected a convoy system for bringing goods from the New World safely to Spain, and for taking Spanish goods back to the New World.

In these ways, the Spanish government made sure that it controlled the territory and people in the New World, and all trade with its Spanish Empire overseas.

Activities

1 Create a mind map showing the connections between Peru and Spain.

2 It is 1530, and Charles I is asking for advice about how the Spanish Empire in the New World should be governed. With a partner, work out what advice you would give him.

3 Put yourself in the shoes of a Spanish merchant. How might he explain to a fellow merchant from England why it is so important that all trade with the New World goes through Seville?

Summary

- Huge amounts of bullion poured into Spain from the 1520s onwards.
- The treasure fleets bringing the bullion to Spain faced many dangers; the Spanish government tried to minimise these dangers by introducing a convoy system.
- Seville became the centre through which all trade to and from the New World had to pass.
- The wealth from the New World was used to buy goods from Europe and Asia, and not to build up Spanish industry and business.
- By 1555, the Spanish government had developed systems to make sure the New World was governed in the way Spain wanted, including the *Casa de Contratacion* (House of Trade) and the Council of the Indies.

Checkpoint

Strengthen

S1 Give one example of the way in which the position of Seville was a strength, and one way in which it was a weakness.

S2 Explain why Seville became such a rich and important city.

S3 Explain how Spanish merchants became involved in the slave trade.

Challenge

C1 Trade with the New World impacted on Spain in several ways. In your own words, summarise three key impacts.

C2 Explain how the *Casa de Contratacion* controlled trade with the New World.

How confident do you feel about your answers to these questions? If you are not certain you answered them well, work in a group, and divide up the tasks so that each person can focus on one aspect in depth before reporting back to the others.

Recap quiz

1 What was the date of Pizarro's third expedition?
2 Who was Huayna Capac?
3 When did smallpox reach Peru?
4 Who led each side in the Inca civil war?
5 Who offered to have a room filled with gold?
6 Where was the Potosi silver mine?
7 What was an *encomendero*?
8 Name the priest who became 'Protector of the Indians'.
9 What did the *Casa de Contratacion* do?
10 What was the name of the city through which all trade with the New World had to pass?

Activities

1 A director is planning to make a short film about Pizarro and his conquest of Peru. Identify the key points in the story that would help with planning in the form of a storyboard.

2 Identify points from the account of Pizarro's conquest of Peru that could be used as examples to support the following statements:

   a Conquistadors viewed the Incas as sub-human.

   b Incas failed to understand the conquistadors' methods and motives.

   c The *encomienda* system aimed to turn the natives into slaves.

3 In a group, discuss the problems created by the New Laws (1542). Were they a reasonable solution to end Spanish exploitation of the Incas? Explain your conclusions.

Exam-style question, Section A

Explain **two** of the following:

* the importance of the murder of Atahuallpa (1533) for Spanish control of Peru
* the importance of the New Laws (1542) for governing the New World
* the importance of the discovery of silver in Potosi (1545) for the Spanish Empire.

16 marks

Exam tip

This question targets your ability to explain the importance of each of the bullet points you choose. Make sure you focus your answer on the difference the event made to the situation given in the bullet point.

Names and Places

Match the following names and places to their definitions below:

Atahuallpa	Inca emperor who died of smallpox
Almagro	Spanish explorer and conquistador who conquered Peru
Huascar	Inca town in Peru where there was a massacre
Huayna Capac	Joint Inca emperor with half-brother
Manco	Inca capital of Peru
Francisco Pizarro	Inca fortress overlooking Cuzco
Cajamarca	Joint Inca emperor with half-brother
Cuzco	Mine where silver was found and a mining town grew up around it
Sacsahuaman	Puppet Inca emperor set up after conquest of Peru
Potosi	Pizarro's business partner and explorer

Writing historically: narrative analysis

When you write a narrative analysis, you need to explain a series of events: their causes and consequences. You need to think about how you express the links between **causes** and **effects**.

Learning outcomes

By the end of this lesson, you will understand how to:

- use conjunctions to link and indicate the relationship between points
- use non-finite verbs to link relevant information or indicate the relationship between points.

Definitions

Co-ordinating conjunction: a word used to link two clauses of equal importance within a sentence, e.g. 'and', 'but', 'so', 'or', etc.

Subordinate clause: a clause that adds detail to or develops the main clause, linked with a subordinating conjunction such as 'because', 'when', 'if', 'although', etc.

How can I link my points in sentences to show cause and effect?

When explaining a complex sequence of events, use **co-ordinating conjunctions** to link them in sentences.

Look at this exam-style narrative analysis task:

> Write a narrative account analysing the key events of 1527–33 that led to the fall of the Inca Empire. **(8 marks)**

1. How could you link these three points using just co-ordinating conjunctions, e.g. 'and', 'but', 'so'?

> In 1527, a smallpox epidemic hit Peru.
> Huayna Capac died, leaving the empire to two of his sons.
> Civil war split the Inca Empire in two.

You can also use **subordinating** conjunctions to make the relationship between cause and effect clear. For example, linking:

- an explanation: (e.g. 'because', 'as', 'in order that', etc.)
- a condition: (e.g. 'if', 'unless', etc.)
- a comparison: (e.g. 'although', 'whereas', 'despite', etc.)
- a sequence: (e.g. 'when', 'as', 'before', 'after', 'until', etc.)

2. Look at these simple, short questions and answers:

   a. Why did Pizarro think he had found a great civilisation in Peru? *He saw glimpses of intricately decorated stone buildings and Ruiz captured elaborate treasures.*

   b. Why did the Inca civil war break out? *Atahuallpa and Huascar were both named as successors to Huayna Capac and both wanted to rule the entire Inca Empire.*

   c. What was the result of the meeting at Cajamarca? *Atahuallpa was captured and many Peruvians killed.*

   d. Why did Atahuallpa offer to fill a room full of gold? *He thought he could bribe the Spaniards from killing him as he knew they wanted gold.*

Rewrite the information in each question and answer as a single sentence. Choose a different type of subordinating conjunction (explanation, condition, comparison and sequence) in each one to express the relationship between cause and effect as clearly as possible.

3. Experiment with different ways of using a subordinating conjunction to link two or more of your sentences into a single sentence.

How can I link my points in other ways?

You can add relevant information and further explanation of cause and effect using **non-finite verbs**. These include: facing / faced, determining / determined, worsening / worsened.

Compare these two extracts, written in response to the exam-style question on the previous page:

> *Atahuallpa agreed to be baptised because he was faced with being burned to death.*

Two points are linked using a subordinating conjunction.

> *Faced with being burned to death, Atahuallpa agreed to be baptised.*

Two points are linked using a non-finite verb.

Look at the two sentences below. How could you link the two points in each one, using a non-finite verb instead of a conjunction? **Hint:** think about how you could use a non-finite form of the highlighted verb.

> *Pizarro was determined to exploit the Inca's weakness, so he pushed on to Cajamarca.*
>
> *Atahuallpa was desperate to live, so he offered to fill a room with gold.*

Did you notice?

There are lots of different ways to link points in sentences. Some of them make the relationship between points more clearly than others.

4. Choose **one** of the sentences above. Experiment with rewriting it in two or three different ways, using different methods to link points. Which version expresses the relationship most clearly and fluently?

Improving an answer

Now look at this paragraph from the beginning of one response to the exam-style narrative analysis task on the previous page:

> *The Inca Empire was large and powerful. In 1527, a smallpox epidemic hit Peru. Thousands died, including Inca Huayna Capac. His death meant that the Empire was divided between two of his sons. Civil war broke out between the brothers and their followers. Pizarro pushed on into Peru, as he was determined to take advantage of a divided empire.*

5. Try rewriting this paragraph, using conjunctions and non-finite verbs to make the sequence of events, and the relationship between cause and effect, clear.

6. Continue the response above with a second paragraph explaining how the situation developed. Use conjunctions and non-finite verbs to make clear connections between causes and effects.

Writing analytical narrative

The difference between a story and a narrative account that analyses

Paper 2, Question 2 will ask you to 'Write a narrative account analysing...' (see page 102 in *Preparing for your exams*). You are not being asked to tell a story in the examination; you are being asked to explain how events led to an outcome. This means showing that the events are a series of happenings that have links between them. To do this, you must show that:

- events are prompted by something
- these events react with other events (or perhaps they react with existing circumstances)
- consequences follow from them.

Showing links like these is what turns a story into 'an account that analyses'.

Narratives for young children are always stories; they deal with events and descriptions. For example, many versions of the adventures of Toad of Toad Hall, originally described in the children's book *The Wind in the Willows*, have been published. These narratives show how Toad got himself into a number of scrapes. One episode describes his fixation with acquiring a fast car, his theft of one, his arrest for dangerous driving and his subsequent trial and imprisonment.

Here are some extracts from *The Wind in the Willows*.

> ### Toad steals a motor car
>
> Toad had a passion for cars. He saw a car in the middle of the yard, quite unattended. Toad walked slowly round it. 'I wonder,' he said to himself, 'if this car starts easily.' Next moment he was turning the starting handle. Then he heard the sound of the engine and, as if in a dream, he found himself in the driver's seat. He drove the car out through the archway and the car leapt forward through the open country...

This extract has the first important ingredient of narrative: sequence – putting events in the right order. Words and phrases like 'next moment' and 'then' show the sequence. However, it lacks the analytical links between events. In this case, key links could be built around phrases such as 'because', 'in order to' or 'as a result of this'.

For example:

> Toad saw the car parked in the middle of the yard. Because there was no one with it, he took the opportunity to have a good look at it. He even gave the starting handle a turn in order to see how easily it started. It started easily, but the sound of the engine affected Toad so much that his old passion for cars resurfaced and his urge to drive the car increased to such an extent that it became irresistible. As a result, as if in a dream, he found himself in the driver's seat...

The analytical narrative, as well as linking events, also makes clear what followed on from them – what difference they made. It uses process words and phrases that show something was happening. In this example, the process words and phrases are 'affected', 'resurfaced', 'increased' and 'became'.

Activities ?

1. Choose a story that you know well – or think of a plot for a story of your own.

2. Select up to eight key events in the story and list them in a sequence. Ideally, these events should be from the beginning, middle and end of the story (if two things happen at the same time you can list them together). Create a flow chart with arrows from one event to the next in the sequence. Label your arrows with links chosen from the chain of linkages (see Figure 1).

3. Write a narrative account analysing the key events of your story. Use the links and at least five process words. Choose them from the process word case (see Figure 2) or use others of your own. Remember that events can combine with long-standing feelings or circumstances as part of the narrative (for example, Toad's passion for motorcars).

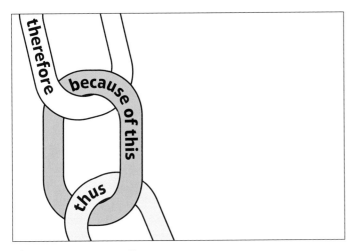

Figure 1 The chain of linkages

Figure 2 Process word case

Writing historical accounts analysing...

You may be asked to write an account that analyses the key events which led to something, or the key events of a crisis, or the way in which something developed. This example has shown the skills you will need to write a good historical account. As you prepare for your examination, you should practise by:

- selecting key events
- sequencing them
- linking them into a process that explains an outcome.

As you study the events of Spain and the 'New World', c1490–c1555, note the linking phrases and process words the author has used in this book. You should add them to your own lists. When you create your own analytical historical narratives, try to make use of both linking phrases and process vocabulary.

Activities ?

Study the timeline on page 50. You can use the events from it to help you to answer the following question: Write a narrative account analysing the key events of Cortes' expedition to Mexico, 1519.

1 With a partner, write the events on pieces of card, without their dates, and then:

   a practise sequencing them correctly

   b agree on another one or two events you could choose to include in your account and any events you could remove

   c identify an instance where long-standing circumstances (or attitudes) were involved as events unfolded.

2 Working individually, write your own narrative account, with linkages and showing a process. Focus on what it is you are explaining and choose process words which relate to, for example, making alliances and conquests.

3 Either swap accounts with a partner or check your own account. Highlight linkages in yellow and process words in green. You can use the same words more than once, but aim to have at least five green and five yellow highlights. See if using more 'process words' improves your account even more.

You are now ready to complete your exam question. Remember to use **SSLaP**.

- **S**elect key events and developments.
- **S**equence them in the right order.
- **L**ink them, **a**nd
- Show the **P**rocess that led to the outcome of your analytical narrative.

Preparing for your GCSE Paper 2 exam

Paper 2 overview

Your Paper 2 is in two sections that examine the Period Study and British Depth Study. They each count for 20% of your History assessment. The questions on Spain and the 'New World' are the Period Study and are in Section A of the exam paper. You should use just under half the time allowed for Paper 2 to write your answers to Section A. This will give a few moments for checking your answers at the end of Section B.

History Paper 2	Period Study and British Depth Study			Time 1 hour 45 mins
Section A	Period Study	Answer 3 questions	32 marks	50 mins
Section B	Depth Options B1 or B2	Answer 3 questions	32 marks	55 mins

Period Study Option 20/21: Spain and the 'New World', c1490–c1555

You will answer Questions 1, 2 and 3.

1 Explain two consequences of... (2 x 4 marks)

Allow 10 minutes to write your answer. Write about each consequence. You are given just over half a page for each. Use this as a guide to answer length. You should keep the answer brief and not try to add more information on extra lines. This will make sure you allow enough time for later questions worth more marks. Make sure you focus on consequence: 'as a result', 'as a consequence' and 'the effect was' are useful phrases to use.

2 Write a narrative account analysing... (8 marks)

This question asks you to write a narrative explaining how events led to an outcome. Allow 15 minutes to write your answer. You are given two information points as prompts to help you. You do not have to use the prompts and you will not lose marks by leaving them out. Always remember to add in a new point of your own as well. Higher marks are gained by adding in a point extra to the prompts. You will be given at least two pages of lines in the answer booklet for your answer. This does not mean you should try to fill all the space. The front page of the exam paper tells you 'there may be more space than you need'. Aim to write an organised answer, putting events in the right order and showing how one connected to the next. Your narrative should have a clear beginning, middle and end.

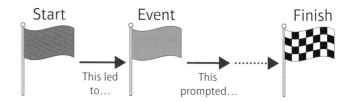

3 Explain the importance of two... (2 x 8 marks)

This question is worth half your marks for the whole Period Study. Make sure you keep 25 minutes of the exam time to answer this. The question asks you to explain the importance of events and developments. You have a choice of two out of three key events. Take time to make the choice. Before you decide, be clear what you have to explain: the question is always worded as 'Explain the importance of... for...' It is a good idea during revision to practise identifying the importance of key events for something: What did they affect or lead to? Ask yourself: 'What difference did they make to it?' or 'Why did they matter?' Be clear about your reasons for saying something is important.

Paper 2 Question 1

Explain **two** consequences of the introduction of the *encomienda* system in the New World. **(8 marks)**

Average answer

Consequence 1

The encomienda system gave land to the Spanish conquistadors who had conquered the New World. It made them settle in places like Haiti and make the land profitable for themselves.

A very general consequence is identified here. There is support given but it shows limited knowledge of the topic. It could be improved with some specific factual detail that focuses on the consequence.

Consequence 2

The encomienda system turned the natives into slaves. They were forced to work for the Spanish men who were running the encomiendas, and were usually treated very cruelly.

A second consequence is identified, but again the supporting evidence is too generalised. It could be improved with more explanation focused on impact.

Verdict

This is an average answer because:

- it identifies two consequences
- it supports each consequence with some general information about the topic.

Use the feedback to rewrite the answer, making as many improvements as you can.

Preparing for your exams

Paper 2 Question 1

Explain **two** consequences of the introduction of the *encomienda* system in the New World. **(8 marks)**

Exam tip

The question wants you to explain the results of something. What difference did it make? Use phrases such as 'as a result' or 'the effect of this was'.

Strong answer

Consequence 1

A consequence of the encomienda system was that the land was worked for the benefit of the Spanish, not the native inhabitants. The Spanish invaders made sure the land was worked for a profit. Because of the need to make the most profit possible, the encomenderos either lived on their encomiendas or, later, in towns nearby so that they could make sure the natives were working hard for them. As a result of this, a stable Spanish society grew up in the New World.

A consequence is clearly identified and is well supported with detail. The use of the phrase 'as a result of' clearly links back to the consequence and shows clear development.

Consequence 2

A feature of the encomienda system was that the natives were forced to pay tribute to the Spanish encomenderos. This tribute was forced from them in goods or labour by the encomenderos, who wanted to make as much profit as possible. The effect of this was that thousands of natives were turned into slaves and many died because of the need to provide tribute to the Spanish. Thousands of natives, for example, died from overwork and malnutrition in the Potosi silver mines. So the consequence of the encomienda system was that it destroyed the natives' way of life and society that had existed before the Spanish invasions.

A second consequence is identified and supported by specific factual detail. The use of phrases like 'the consequence of' and 'the effect of this' keeps the explanation focused on consequence.

Verdict

This is a strong answer because:
- it identifies two different consequences
- it supports each consequence with specific detail
- the explanation focuses on consequence.

Paper 2 Question 2

Write a narrative account analysing the key events of 1527–33 that led to the fall of the Inca Empire.

You may use the following in your answer:

- the death of Huayna Capac (1527)

- the Battle of Cajamarca (1532).

You **must** also use information of your own. **(8 marks)**

Average answer

Before 1527, Pizarro had made two expeditions to Peru. Although he found gold, the expeditions were unsuccessful. He had problems finding funding for his third expedition, but it was eventually authorised by King Charles I.

This introduction uses accurate information but it would be improved with a clear link to the question.

A smallpox epidemic hit Peru in December 1527 and the leader of the Incas, Huayna Capac, died. Civil war then broke out between his sons. This was won by Atahuallpa, who defeated his half-brother, Huascar.

This is correct information but it is not linked to the question to make an explained account.

In 1531, Pizarro landed in Ecuador and marched south into Peru. In 1532, the Spaniards attacked Atahuallpa and the Incas in the town of Cajamarca. They captured Atahuallpa. He offered them a room full of gold in return for his release. The Incas filled the room with gold, but the Spaniards still killed Atahuallpa, and then the Spaniards were able to take over the Inca Empire.

The answer is organised, as it is in chronological order. While the final sentence links back to the question, the answer would be improved by showing the links between each of the relevant events.

Verdict

This is an average answer because:

- the information is mostly relevant, completely accurate and in the correct chronological order

- it lacks sufficient explanatory links to show the connections between events

- it does not show how the events led to the fall of the Inca Empire.

Use the feedback to rewrite the answer, making as many improvements as you can.

Paper 2 Question 2

Write a narrative account analysing the key events of 1527–33 that led to the fall of the Inca Empire.
You may use the following in your answer:

- the death of Huayna Capac (1527)

- the Battle of Cajamarca (1532).

You **must** also use information of your own. **(8 marks)**

Strong answer

At the beginning of 1527, the Inca Empire was large and powerful. It was strengthened by the thousands of Inca warriors who conquered and then subdued all other tribes. The powerful Inca Huayna Capac ruled over the empire with a mixture of cruelty, drive and determination.

The answer begins well. It establishes the situation in 1527 and provides a good starting point for beginning an explanation about the fall of the Inca Empire.

Suddenly, in 1527, three years before Pizarro landed in South America, a smallpox epidemic hit Peru. This resulted in the death of thousands, including Huayna Capac. His death meant that the empire was divided between two of his sons, Atahuallpa and Huascar. The arrangement worked well for a short time and then civil war broke out between the brothers and their followers, weakening the empire. Although Atahuallpa won the civil war, the Incas were divided in their loyalties and this resulted in the empire remaining weak.

This paragraph links events together with connectives and information showing an understanding of the change brought about by the smallpox epidemic.

Pizarro took advantage of this divided empire. When he landed in Ecuador in 1531, it meant that he was able to march straight down to the Peruvian town of Cajamarca unopposed. A weakened Inca force resulted in Atahuallpa welcoming Pizarro and his men. The treacherous Spaniards attacked Atahuallpa and the Incas in the square in the middle of Cajamarca. Taken by surprise, the Incas were defeated; Pizarro, determined to take personal control of a chaotic situation, captured Atahuallpa and imprisoned him in a small room. Atahuallpa offered Pizarro a room full of gold in exchange for his life. Cunning and deceitful, Pizarro agreed. This agreement resulted in the Inca people, anxious to save their leader, gradually filling the room with gold. Once it was full, Pizarro, a ruthless liar, had Atahuallpa killed. The death of Atahuallpa meant that the Inca Empire collapsed.

This paragraph introduces the personality of Pizarro into the explained account and continues with signposting the analysis by the use of phrases such as 'resulted in' and 'meant that'.

Verdict

This is a strong answer because:

- the information is relevant, accurate and shows a good understanding of events

- it gives explanatory links to show the connections between events

- it has a coherent line of reasoning to show how the events led to the fall of the Inca Empire.

Paper 2 Question 3

Explain **two** of the following:

- The importance of the settlement at La Navidad (1492) for Spanish exploration of the New World. **(8 marks)**
- The importance of the capture of Tenochtitlan (1521) for the growth of the Spanish Empire. **(8 marks)**
- The importance of the New Laws (1542) for Spanish control of the New World. **(8 marks)**

One event is demonstrated below as an example, but your answer would need to include a discussion of a **second** event as well.

Exam tip

You are not asked to describe the event, but to explain its importance. Think about its significance. What did it lead to or change? What difference did it make?

Average answer

- The importance of the settlement at La Navidad (1492) for Spanish exploration of the New World. **(8 marks)**

La Navidad was built from the timbers of Columbus' flag ship, the Santa Maria. It had been wrecked off the coast of Haiti on Christmas Eve 1492. Columbus had to build the settlement because he only had one ship left, the Nina, and it wasn't big enough to take all the Spanish soldiers back to Spain. La Navidad was the first European settlement in the New World.

La Navidad was one of the reasons for Columbus' second expedition. He had to rescue the Spaniards he had left behind. When Columbus reached La Navidad in November 1493, however, he found it burnt to the ground and all the Spaniards had been killed. The natives had wiped out the first European settlement. This was the start of the hatred between the Spaniards and the natives of the New World.

All the information in this paragraph is accurate. However, it needs to be more sharply focused on the question, which asks about the importance of the settlement. This is giving the reasons why it was built, which is not what the question is asking.

The first two sentences hint at the importance of La Navidad, as does the last one. However, the rest of the paragraph describes what happened. This needs to be much more firmly linked to the significance of the settlement for Spanish exploration of the New World.

Verdict

This is an average answer because:
- the information about La Navidad and Columbus is accurate, showing some knowledge and understanding of the period
- it does not explain importance enough to be a strong answer
- there is some development of points, but the line of reasoning is not always clear. The link to Spanish exploration of the New World is not made clear.

Use the feedback to rewrite this answer, making as many improvements as you can.

Paper 2 Question 3

Explain **two** of the following:

- The importance of the settlement at La Navidad (1492) for Spanish exploration of the New World. **(8 marks)**

- The importance of the capture of Tenochtitlan (1521) for the growth of the Spanish Empire. **(8 marks)**

- The importance of the New Laws (1542) for Spanish control of the New World. **(8 marks)**

One event is demonstrated below as an example, but your answer would need to include a discussion of a **second** event as well.

Exam tip

You are not asked to describe the event, but to explain its importance. Think about its significance. What did it lead to or change? What difference did it make?

Strong answer

- The importance of the settlement at La Navidad (1492) for Spanish exploration of the New World. **(8 marks)**

The building of La Navidad was important because it was the first indication that the Spaniards were in the New World to stay and that they would therefore explore further. The wrecking of the Santa Maria and the disappearance of Martin Pinzon with the Pinta meant that only the Nina was left to sail back to Spain and it wasn't large enough to take them all. Columbus negotiated with the friendly Tainos natives for permission to build a settlement for the people he was going to leave behind, and the settlement was built with their help from the timbers of the Santa Maria. The natives at this point were friendly, making any decisions about further exploration likely to be positive.

The building of La Navidad was important to Columbus because he wanted to explore more in the New World. He could use the need to return on a rescue expedition as an argument for a second expedition. However, when he did get back to La Navidad in November 1493, it had been burned to the ground and there was no trace of the Spaniards that had been left behind.

The settlement at La Navidad was not only important to Columbus. It was important, too, for all further Spanish exploration in the New World because it showed that, while some native tribes were friendly, others were not and resented the entry of the Spanish into their world. The first Spanish settlement, first agreed to by the natives, had been wiped out by them. What happened at La Navidad made the Spanish determined to continue exploring the New World but, at the same time, to regard the natives as enemies.

The importance of the settlement at La Navidad is explained as an indication of Spanish intentions and the information given is accurate and directed at the question.

A clear focus on the question is maintained and the link made between Columbus and further Spanish exploration is made.

The importance of La Navidad for future Spanish exploration of the New World is clearly explained and the link back to the question firmly made. Throughout, the line of reasoning is clear and the answer well-structured.

Verdict

This is a strong answer because:

- information is accurate, showing good knowledge and understanding of the importance of La Navidad

- the explanation shows an analysis of both short-term and long-term importance

- the line of reasoning is coherent and well-structured.

Answers to Recall Quiz questions

Chapter 1

1 August 1492
2 King Ferdinand and Queen Isabella of Spain
3 The *Pinta*, the *Nina* and the *Santa Maria*
4 To find a sea route to the Spice Islands by sailing west across the Atlantic
5 A native tribe living on Haiti
6 It agreed that lands to the west of an imaginary line drawn from the North Pole to the South Pole, were to be Spanish; and to the east, Portuguese
7 Francisco de Bobadilla
8 *Casa de Contratacion*
9 Antonio de Montesinos
10 December 1512

Chapter 2

1 1513
2 Santa Maria de la Antigua del Darien
3 Hatuey
4 Velázquez
5 September 1522
6 He captained the only ship in Magellan's expedition to circumnavigate the world
7 The Aztec emperor
8 Tenochtitlan
9 13 August 1521
10 The Aztec Empire (centred on Mexico)

Chapter 3

1 December 1530
2 The Inca (ruler) of the Inca people
3 December 1527
4 Atahuallpa and Huascar
5 Atahuallpa
6 The Cerro Rico mountain, in the centre of what is now Bolivia
7 A Spaniard in charge of an *encomienda*
8 Bartolome de las Casas
9 Controlled all trade between Spain and the New World
10 Seville

Index

Key terms are capitalised initially, in bold type with an asterisk.
Headings for topic booklets are shown in *italics*.

Acknowledgements
Picture Credits

The publisher would like to thank the following for their kind permission to reproduce their photographs:

(Key: b-bottom; c-centre; l-left; r-right; t-top)

123RF.com: ildipapp 89; **akg-images Ltd:** 23, De Agostini Picture Lib. 62, De Agostini Picture Lib. / G. Dagli Orti 54t, THEODOR DE BRY 13; **Alamy Stock Photo:** classicpaintings 68, 95, Granger Historical Picture Archive 38, 40, HimageBROKER 32; **Bridgeman Art Library Ltd:** Academia das Ciencias de Lisboa, Lisbon, Portugal / De Agostini Picture Library / M. Seemuller 83, Private Collection / Archives Charmet 44, Private Collection / Look and Learn 24, Private Collection / Photo © Christie's Images 76, Universal History Archive / UIG 52; **Getty Images:** Hulton Archive 94, Spanish School 57; **John Carter Brown Library:** Courtesy of the John Carter Brown Library at Brown University 27; **Mary Evans Picture Library:** 19, 29, CAGP / Iberfoto 8, 15; **Shutterstock.com:** Lukasz Kurbiel 73; **SuperStock:** Iberfoto 4, 60; **TopFoto:** Fine Art Images / Heritage Images 9, The Granger Collection 54b

Cover images: *Front:* **Bridgeman Art Library Ltd:** Museo degli Argenti, Palazzo Pitti, Florence, Italy / De Agostini Picture Library / A. Dagli Orti

All other images © Pearson Education

We are grateful to the following for permission to reproduce copyright material:

Text
Extract in Interpretation 1 on page 24 from *Columbus: The Four Voyages, 1492-1504* by Laurence Bergreen. Used by permission of Viking Books, an imprint of Penguin Publishing; Group, a division of Penguin Random House LLC. All rights reserved; Extracts in Interpretation 1 on page 28 and in Interpretation 2 on page 48 from *Rivers of Gold: the Rise of the Spanish Empire*, from Columbus to Magellan by Hugh Thomas, copyright © 2003. Used by permission of Random House, an imprint and division of Penguin Random House LLC. All rights reserved; Extracts in Interpretation 1 on page 42 and in Interpretation 1 on page 84 from *The Spanish Seaborne Empire* by John Horace Parry, 1966. Used by permission of Random House, an imprint and division of Penguin Random House and LLC. All rights reserved; Extract in Interpretation 1 on page 57 from *Conquistador: Hernan Cortes, King Montezuma, and the Last Stand of the Aztecs,* by Buddy Levy, coyright © 2008 by Buddy Levy. Used by permission of Bantam Books, an imprint of Random House, a division of Penguin Random House LLC. All rights reserved; Extract in Interpretation 1 on page 72 and in Interpretation 2 on page 77 from *Conquistadors*, BBC Books (Wood,M with permission from Random House Group UK.